Satan Is Here.
God Is Coming!

Leon Kelly Jr.

KellyHead

Published by KellyHead Publishing Group, a division of KellyHead Multimedia.

For information about permission to reproduce any part of this book, email: permission@kellyheadmultimedia.com

All scripture quotations are taken from the King James Version of the Bible (Public Domain).

Cover design by: Jason Orr @ Jera Publishing, LLC

Publisher's Cataloging-in-Publication Data
Kelly, Leon, Jr., 1967-
Satan Is Here. God Is Coming! / Leon Kelly, Jr.
pages cm

ISBN-13: 9780977905041 (pbk.)
ISBN-10: 0977905047

ISBN-13: 978-0-9779050-7-2 (e-book)
ISBN-10: 0-9779050-7-1

Devil—Christianity. Good and evil—Religious aspects—Christianity.
Revelation—Christianity. Prophecy—Christianity. Spiritual warfare.
RELIGION / Christian Life / Spiritual Warfare.

BT982.K45 2017
235/.47—dc23

2016913462

Dedication

To God the Father, who created me in His image.
To Jesus Christ the Son, who died for my sins.
To the Holy Spirit, who comforts and guides me.
To the angels appointed to watch over me.
To every earthly "angel" who has ever shown up
in my life.

Contents

1
Who Is Satan?

EVERY BEING AND everything has a beginning. The only exception to that statement is God, because God alone is "the beginning and the ending" (Rev. 1:8). God is omnipotent (He has all power in His hands), omnipresent (He is everywhere at the same time), and omniscient (He knows everything there is to know). God alone is always everywhere, possessing all power and knowledge. "In the beginning God created the heaven and the earth" (Gen. 1:1). God is the Creator and owner of all things: of heaven, earth, man, woman, every tree, every animal, every bird, and everything else in existence. "And God saw every thing that he had made, and, behold, it was very good. And the evening and the morning were the sixth day" (v. 31). Everything was complete: "the heavens and the earth were finished, and all the host of them" (2:1).

The angels were created too, though we do not know exactly when. However, according to scripture, we are told that they witnessed God's work—some of it, anyway. When we read chapter 38 of Job, we find out that the angels were there, looking on, while God was in the midst of creating the earth. God spoke to Job, asking his servant, "Where wast thou when I laid the foundations of the earth?" (v. 4). Then He asked Job where he was "when the morning stars sang together, and all the sons of God shouted for joy" (v. 7).

The angels—called "the sons of God" in Job 38:7—cheered God during the creation. What an awesome thing it must have been to bear witness to the magnificent works of God! That had to be something special. God made man "a little lower than the angels" (Ps. 8:5); nevertheless, the angels were shouting for joy during the creation of man. God created the angels to "do his commandments, hearkening unto the voice of his word" (103:20). And in regard to man, scripture says, "For he shall give his angels charge over thee, to keep thee in all thy ways" (91:11). The angels are watching over us. It is God's command. They were created to do God's will and to do good always. However, some angels have refused to follow God's commands!

Evil has a beginning. One angel who was there watching the great works of God was "Lucifer, son of the morning" (Isa. 14:12). This angel was the brightest star. He held the highest position of any of the angels in heaven. Lucifer was God's "anointed cherub," who "wast upon the holy mountain of God" (Ezek. 28:14). Lucifer "wast perfect" in his ways from the day he was created until iniquity was found in him (Ezek. 28:15). The son of morning said that he would "ascend above the heights of the clouds" and "be like the most High" (Isa. 14:14).

Examining the scriptures, we see that the star angel—the anointed one, the perfect angel, the one who walked around in the presence of God—was found to possess a sinful disposition. Having been in the presence of all that was good, the son of the morning began to possess evil desires. God said to Lucifer, "Thine heart was lifted up because of thy beauty, thou hast corrupted thy wisdom by reason of thy brightness" (Ezek. 28:17). From that point on, the son of the morning lost his light. He became as the darkness because he walked outside the counsel of the Almighty. He is the first and chief fallen angel.

Satan, the former angel of light, has many names according to the Living Word, which is the gospel, the truth, and the inspired Word of God. Satan is many things, and depending on the person he is trying to conquer, he is able to become whatever he needs to be to win someone over. As we will see in this chapter, numerous scriptures point out who and what Satan is. These scriptures also point out his shady characteristics. The Bible, our book of instruction or spiritual road map on how to live this life, speaks extensively on the character of the evil one. As we will discover, the devil is here in a big way. He plays various roles, possesses traits rooted in evil, and is closer to us than we may realize. Satan and his army of fallen angels are here to stay until the end. In our lifetimes we can expect to have some run-ins with evil. So to know the devil and his camp and be prepared for them is to be able to resist and overcome the fiery darts of evil.

For starters the evil one is referred to as "the great dragon ... that old serpent, called the Devil, and Satan" (Rev. 12:9). Notice the word "great." The great dragon is among us, and he is filled with rage and armed with a significant amount of power. We are also warned that Satan possesses great anger (Rev. 12:12). Reason being: his existence on earth is about to come to an end, and his punishment of eternal damnation is about to be handed down. He wants so desperately to take out his anger on us. He will do whatever is needed to get close enough to us to cause irreparable damage. The serpent will use human beings to trap and deceive other human beings. If we let him into our hearts, he will make us part of his army.

The serpent has a considerable amount of influence. He is not to be taken lightly. Satan is real. And he is here—on earth—and he did not come alone. Satan "was cast out into the earth, and his angels were cast out with him" (Rev. 12:9). The demonic forces that fell from heaven with Satan are working to secure every soul to the furthering of the kingdom of darkness. The devil and his demonic forces are watching us, figuring out ways to win us over to the side of evil. That is their job—all day, every day.

The devil will probably never walk up to us and tell us who he is. His army of demons may not introduce themselves as angels of death. During our first few dealings with Satan, it is possible that we will be fooled. The devil can sneak up on us undetected. He did it to Eve in the Garden of Eden. Satan knows exactly how to use us to ruin a good thing. After God had instructed Eve and Adam not to eat from the tree that would expose them to the knowledge of good and evil—because they would then die—the serpent approached Eve in a cool, calm, and collected manner. As Genesis 3:1 states, "the serpent was more subtil than any beast of the field which the LORD God had made." Satan is the master of sneaky. He is also the master of disguise. He can take upon himself any image he desires. That is what makes him so dangerous.

Satan sweet-talked his way into Eve's life. She accepted his word over the Creator's instructions forbidding her and Adam to touch, or eat the fruit of, the tree in the middle of the garden. Satan told Eve, "Ye shall not surely die: For God doth know that in the day ye eat thereof, then your eyes shall be opened, and ye shall be as gods, knowing good and evil" (vv. 4-5). Here we see Satan the liar. And, boy oh boy, can he tell a smooth one! The serpent provided what proved to be a tempting proposition. Eve, from the looks of it, found the idea of being like a god and possessing the knowledge of good and evil more appealing than having access to an abundance of goodness.

God gave Adam and Eve a multitude of trees from which to eat. They only had to obey him by staying away from one tree: "the tree of the knowledge of good and evil" (2:17). But Eve wanted more, and the devil certainly knew it. Armed with his awareness of Eve's curiosity, the serpent set the trap, and Eve took the bait. Being persuaded by the serpent, Eve bought into the lies of the devil. She then convinced Adam to eat the forbidden fruit. That is how sneaky and cunning the devil is. He must have known that if he tricked the woman, she would have enough power to trick the man. And he was right. The devil lied, and Adam and Eve believed him. This is the first documented lie.

In the book of Genesis, we see the old serpent as the full-fledged liar that he is. He deceived the first humans on earth. His ability to deceive seemed effortless. With his elaborate lie, the devil deceived the woman into believing that she and Adam would not die—that they would be as gods! Satan was actually calling God a liar. Scripture teaches that "God is not a man, that He should lie" (Num. 23:19). One of Satan's most devastating strengths is twisting the truth. Jesus said the devil "abode not in the truth, because there is no truth in him" (John 8:44). In the same verse Jesus continued to explain what the devil does and who he is, saying, "When he speaketh a lie, he speaketh of his own: for he is a liar, and the father of it." We should have no doubt about who the devil is. God tells us who he is: Satan is the father of lies. We must remember that the devil always wants to deceive us into believing the lies he and his agents tell.

Why? Because lies have the power to destroy. Millions of people have bought into the devil's lies. He and his willing agents have destroyed countless lives with their lies. It is no wonder Jesus also called Satan "a murderer from the beginning" in John 8:44. Satan is both the father of lies and a murderer. His lying tongue and murderous ways are able to reach near and far. His agents of death make that possible. They spread his poison throughout the earth.

The embarrassment of lies has caused many a man, woman, and child to take their own life. Lies have so much power to destroy because the devil, through lies, is able to make them appear so great that we cannot possibly overcome them. It is difficult enough for believers to get over the pain of a lie. For people who are already doubting the existence of God, a lie can easily be the end of their lives. They would rather take their own lives than to live with the damage a lie could do to their reputation. That old, cunning serpent had a plan back in the Garden of Eden, and—what do you know—that plan still works. Satan is the beginning of evil.

Satan, the evil one, and his angels wear different hats. They are our next-door neighbors. They are employed in decision-making roles at local, national, and federal levels. Angels of darkness occupy space in every corner of the universe. They are cooks and servers at our favorite restaurants. Demons reside in the hearts of our classmates and "friends." They are heads of states and companies. Demons are a part of our team. We have partied with them and sat beside them in church. We have dated and/or slept with evil. We have interviewed with evil. We have worked with evildoers, who are sons and daughters of the devil. Angels of darkness have shaken our hands, smiled at us, and given us a pat on the back. And for those of us who believe we have never met Satan or his demons, it's possible we just might be a son or daughter of the devil.

Satan is many things. He wears every hat, meaning he is everything—at least everything that is evil. And his evil influence is everywhere. Satan is the exact opposite of God in his nature. God is love. Satan is hatred. He is the head of evildoers, the people who possess his spirit. People, please know that Satan has not come in the flesh. We cannot see him. Satan is a spiritual being. While we may refer to certain human beings as the devil or Satan, the father of lies is neither human nor visible to the human eye. Ephesians 6:12 explains it like this: "For we wrestle not against flesh and blood, but against principalities, against powers, against the rulers of the darkness of this world, against spiritual wickedness in high places." Human beings are merely Satan's vessels, those of us who are willing to allow Satan to take up residence in our hearts and minds, and to carry out unspeakable evils against mankind.

Satan is a father, a husband, a son, and a brother. He is a wife, a mother, a sister, or a daughter. He is a relative and a neighbor. He is a teacher, a student, a preacher, a deacon, a choir member, a church member. He is a judge, a lawyer, a police officer, a member of the armed forces, a so-called friend, a missionary, an employee, an employer, a doctor, a nurse, a counselor, a psychologist, a psychiatrist, a politician, and an expert on many things. If there is any hat to be worn,

Satan wears it. Most often he comes in sheep's clothing, pretending to have our best interests at heart. That's how he is able to fool people who have no clue who God is, and to cause so much devastation in the world. Of course he works through those individuals he possesses.

Satan is "the god of this world" (2 Cor. 4:4). I will later speak more in depth on the power of the world's god to blind the minds of unbelievers. For now, however, I simply want you to know that Satan is the god of this world, and as such we are not to love the world. The following scriptures refer to Satan as "the prince of this world": John 12:31, John 14:30, and John 16:11. The prince of this world has his hands on every evil thing that happens. And because the majority of humanity remains enslaved to sin, we will witness all sorts of evil, even great evil that is yet to come. In our fallen state Satan has great power to persuade and influence us. To give in to his power of influence is a costly mistake. To avoid his trickery is wisdom.

Another one of Satan's names is "Beelzebub," and he is "the chief of the devils" (Luke 11:15). As the prince of this world and the chief of all demons, Satan plants his angels where they are most impactful and where they are able to cause the most harm. Make no mistake about it: Satan and his devils have their hands in every injustice, every act of malice, discrimination, deception, and hypocrisy. The Bible informs us that in the children of Satan there is no righteousness and that those who commit sin are the devil's children (1 John 3:8, 10). He and his gatekeepers (those who are ready and willing to divide and to destroy in the name of their father, the devil) are everywhere, infecting human beings and distorting the truth. For the time being, Satan is looking out for his own and protecting his own.

We can deny him power over our lives all day long by rebuking him in the name of Jesus, but we must first recognize him, which means recognizing that the prince of this world is great in his influence. Then we must realize that by partaking in sin, we weaken ourselves and our power to overcome the devil. When we walk in the spirit of sin, which means we have turned away from God, we are living a life contrary to His teachings. It means we are walking in the spirit of the world, which is "according to the prince of the power of the air" (Eph. 2:2). It is the same "spirit that now worketh in the children of disobedience: Among whom also we all had our conversation in times past in the lusts of our flesh, fulfilling the desires of the flesh and of the mind; and were by nature the children of wrath, even as others" (Eph. 2:2-3). Again, this shows Satan's power to influence the way we think about sin.

Satan is "the angel of the bottomless pit" (Rev. 9:11). Can you imagine what the bottomless pit—also called hell—looks like? It is a dark place, a place of torment, and those who inhabit such a place are never able to find peace. It is ruled over by the destroyer of men's souls. It is ugly and scary. No light shines through. Only suffering exists there. Satan is the king and the merciless overseer of this bottomless pit, which is the eternal dwelling of those who live apart from God. The head of unrepentant sinners will delight forever in the suffering of those he deceived while they were yet inhabitants of the earth. He will destroy souls, just like the souls of the Israelites who turned away from God and turned to sin. In 1 Corinthians 10:10, it says they "were destroyed of the destroyer."

Satan is an accuser. Revelations 12:10 says "for the accuser of our brethren is cast down, which accused them before our God day and night." The serpent is forever falsely accusing people of wrongdoings, especially when he is trying to hide his hand. Have you ever been accused of something you did not do but still have many people against you because of the accusations? I definitely have, to the point that for a long while I believed my life was over. It filled me with suicidal thoughts. Being falsely accused of a crime or a sin is an awful feeling. It causes so much pain and threatens to drain life from the body. Many people have taken their own lives because of false accusations. That is exactly what the accuser wants.

Satan is our adversary. He is stalking us and trying to overtake us, especially during times when we are unaware. So "be sober, be vigilant; because your adversary the devil, as a roaring lion, walketh about, seeking whom he may devour" (1 Pet. 5:8). Satan is not our friend. The old serpent is against us. He wants nothing more than to oppose us at every turn. When things are going our way, he will come in and shake things up; he'll put obstacles in our path. The adversary is a hostile force who will, for example, oppose us for advocating peace. He will hate us for telling the truth. He will step into our lives and work diligently to tear down what we have built. He envies the success of others and will argue convincingly why we do not deserve to have what we have. He will persuade likeminded beings—people with malice in their hearts—to join him in tearing down what we have worked hard to build. He will stop at nothing to see us fall. It happens all the time. I am certain we can all think of times when the adversary made his case against us.

The devil, our enemy, is at war with us. He is at war with peace. He is an enemy who shows up in friendly disguises, but he wants nothing good to happen to us or for us. The enemy does not want us to get along with one another. The enemy will come during the noisiest times in our lives, when we have so much going on with work, school, or family matters that we may be too exhausted to put forth a little more effort to pay attention to what is going on around us. It's at those times when the enemy is at his most destructive.

When we find ourselves at the crossroads of doubt and desperation, the devil swoops in and tempts us with the fleshly desires of our hearts. The enemy of men is a tempter in every sense of the word. Satan tempted Jesus after He had been in the wilderness for forty days. The Bible provides record of the devil and his attempt to get Jesus to bow down to him: "And he was there in the wilderness forty days, tempted of Satan" (Mark 1:13). Matthew 4:3 testifies, "And when the tempter came to him, he said, If thou be the Son of God, command that these stones be made bread." Satan already knew who Jesus was. He knew that Jesus had been sent to defeat him. But the devil still put forth his best effort to get Jesus to cave. If Satan had the audacity to tempt Jesus, do not for one second think he is not out here in the world, tempting us by promising us what our hearts desire.

Without hesitation the devil and his crew will grant us our desires if we follow them. Satan will wait until we are hanging at the end of our ropes. That is when he will present himself, offering us our worldly desires. He knows our weaknesses. He will promise us access to whatever we want in this world, just like he did Jesus. The devil showed Jesus "all the kingdoms of the world, and the glory of them" (v. 8). Then the tempter made Jesus a conditional offer, saying, "All these things will I give thee, if thou wilt fall down and worship me" (v. 9). Satan went there. Yes he did! He felt no shame in his crooked game. Satan, being the prince of this world, is equipped to make our wildest dreams come true. But there is a condition. The tempter is saying to us, "If you work for me and worship me, I will give you whatever you want." It is called signing a deal with the devil. There is much temporary gain. But the price of such temporary gain is costly. The price is death: a second death—spiritual death.

Although countless people refuse to believe Satan exists, he is real, and he is present. They see the devil as some mythical creature. As a matter of fact, some people see God like they see Santa Claus. I've had one person who let me know he viewed God just like he thought of Santa Claus. This man, a coworker, noticed my Bible on my desk, so he pointed to it and asked, "Do you believe in the Bible?" I told him that I believe in the Bible wholeheartedly. He looked me in my eyes and, with a half-cocked smile, said that he did not believe in God and that he thought of God as a make-believe character. I never told him that he was wrong to believe what he believes. I simply stated that I could not imagine how my life would have any meaning without my belief in God.

If people do not believe in God, what reason would they have to believe that Satan exists? There is no real answer to that question. However, the Bible clearly tells us the devil exists. To believe he does not exist is exactly what he wants. He is at his most destructive when we do not believe he exists. It is like walking through a forest barefoot, carefree, and unsuspecting—and suddenly being bitten by a deadly viper hiding in the tall grass. That snake in the grass is Satan. He is sneaky and deceptive. He slithers through the grass, hiding, adapting, and blending in with his surroundings. By the time we realize he exists and we see the deadliness of his power, it is oftentimes too late. It happens every day to unsuspecting people, because they are never prepared for something they believe does not exist.

Here are a few important things to remember about Satan:

He is real.
He is inferior to God.
He will not and cannot have the final say.
He can only use us to do his dirty work if we are willing.
He can be anyone or anything except God.
God gave us power over him.
He is already defeated.

Satan might be the god of this world, but he is *not* God. Satan cannot do anything without God's permission. The most important thing to remember is that when Jesus died on the cross for our sins, He defeated Satan. So Satan knows what his end is. Thus he will stop at nothing to separate us from living eternally with God. The devil only has as much power over us as we give him. If we don't give him power to reign supreme in our lives, he cannot claim our eternal souls.

2
Works of the Devil

THE WORK OF the devil is sin. Satan is sin. He sinned from the beginning of time and quite possibly before time itself. He is the father of sin. His children glory in sin. Sin is the devil's way of rebelling against God. He knows that sin is at odds with God, and he would like to continue his work of blinding the minds of mankind so that we will adopt sin as a good and acceptable way of life. The enemy is aware that when we are in the midst of our sins, we become disconnected from God and become his children rather than God's.

Unfortunately the great deceiver has used his influence to deceive human beings into thinking they are righteous and without sin. The Bible sets the record straight, teaching that "as by one man sin entered into the world, and death by sin; and so death passed upon all men, for that all have sinned" (Rom. 5:12). The truth is, we are all sinners in need of forgiveness and mercy. Yet people go about their daily lives rebelling against the Creator and neglecting to ask for forgiveness, because, in their eyes, they have done nothing wrong. They can no longer see the sins they commit. Romans 3:23 paints a clear picture of us in relation to sin: "For all have sinned, and come short of the glory of God." Did you notice the word "all"?

Some people adopt a holier-than-thou attitude and refuse to admit they are sinners. But "if we say that we have no sin, we deceive ourselves, and the truth is not in us" (1 John 1:8). First John 1:10 further explains that "if we say that we have not sinned, we make him a liar, and his word is not in us." If you are ever in the company of individuals who claim they are above sin or have no sin in them, know that you are in the presence of liars who do not have the Word of God in them. It is not a judgment call. You are simply using scripture to identify those who have nothing in common with the truth.

Society is typically more accepting of one group of sinners over other groups of sinners, because human beings rank sin. When man yells that one sin is greater than another, God has already proven that to be a lie. Usually the public goes on the attack against certain sinners while remaining neutral and less active against other sinners, in part because they may not believe that certain sins are actually sins at all. This is evident everywhere. I challenge you to look around, to observe the sins that are attacked more passionately than others. For the sake of example, take homosexuality. It is a sin. There is no arguing that biblical truth—and believing the Word of God is not a form of hate speech.

When someone says, "Homosexuality is wrong," and then uses the scripture to back it up, he is not attacking the homosexual. He is stating the truth according to the Word of God. Telling the truth is not inviting others to hate the sinner. The gospel is, if believed and adhered to, medicine to the soul. I think what confuses people the most is that too many of us hate the sinner and attack the sinner with such venom that it doesn't heal or invite the sinner to repent, but it puts a bad taste in the sinner's mouth for anything having to do with God or the Bible.

We are all sinners. The original nature of humans is sin. King David realized that man is a sinner from birth: "Behold, I was shapen in iniquity; and in sin did my mother conceive me" (Ps. 51:5). When we come into the world, we come as sinners and the world itself is filled with iniquity. To have a leaning toward a certain sin (or sins) is in all of us. However, we do not have to partake in any sin just because we feel an urge to act upon it. Kind David had eyes for a married woman named Bathsheba. He lusted for her and then engaged in sexual relations with her. To cover up for these sins, David also had murder in his heart and wanted Bathsheba's husband to die in battle. David knew his behavior was sinful and admitted as much. He took full ownership of his sinful ways. God was merciful to him, and He will show us mercy, but first we have to admit that we have rebelled against God by engaging in sinful behavior.

It is difficult for most people who live with this homosexuality to accept it as sexually immoral. To the sinner in denial, it is normal behavior and is just as natural as a marriage (notice, I said *marriage*) between a man and a woman. It is not. The flesh is offended by the truth, because the practitioner of this sinful behavior does not understand that we must die to the flesh daily. That means we must make sacrifices for God. If we are inclined to a particular sin, we are to resist, with everything in us, the urge to sin, although that sin might give us temporary pleasures. Giving up such unnatural affections and lusts is what God commands. The Bible states, "And they that are Christ's have crucified the flesh with the affections and lusts" (Gal. 5:24). With the gospel truth having been stated, let me get back to the point of using homosexuality as an example of one of those sins that causes so much uproar.

Much of the world is up in arms over homosexuality and gay marriage. Believers should be against this and all other sinful behaviors. But that is not the case. I think we could all agree that homosexuality is the most protested sexual sin in this era. You do not hear of business owners refusing to serve an adulterer, a fornicator, or any other sinner like they do the homosexual. You would think it is the worst sin that a person could commit. Many people are outraged over same-sex marriage and same-sex relationships, so much that they allow hatred to build in them and to boil over, sometimes to the point of committing hate crimes. It speaks to the deceit of people's hypocrisy.

Committing a sin against someone because we do not like the sin he or she is committing goes to show that most of us do not have the truth in us. All sin is against God. He weighs all sins equally. All sin, if we do not turn away from it, leads to death, "for the wages of sin is death" (Rom. 6:23). Please know that this means if we continue in our sin, we will be sentenced to an eternal death. It does not mean that we are to go out and kill people for sinning.

Moreover homosexuality is often blamed for the fall of the family, the reason 9-11 happened, and the reason for the collapse of the world, among other things. Those are beliefs shared by many, even world-renown religious leaders who should know better. I'm not making this up. Some ministers and televangelists have actually made such statements blaming homosexuals. It is pure ignorance to blame every bad thing that happens on the sin of homosexuality. Individuals in tune with God's truth know that the collapse of this world is due to ALL sin. It is due to our rejection of God as the Supreme Being. And the collapse of the family is also due to all kinds of sin, with adultery being at the top of the list. We must encourage others to forsake all sin, not just the one sin we hate with a passion. We are charged with teaching the whole truth, not a portion of it.

If you ask around, you'll get varying answers as to what sin is. People frequently name every sin except the one sin that brings them the most pleasure. It is a move straight out of Satan's playbook. I don't argue about sin with people. I simply tell them what the Bible says. When I do this, I often find that I am the object of contempt. It used to frustrate me when people would get angry with me for believing what the Bible says is sin. But as I grow in the knowledge of God, I can identify people who have allowed Satan to deceive them.

Drug users and alcoholics believe that doing drugs and overindulging in alcohol are pastimes that are somehow okay. Individuals who engage in same-sex behavior believe that God made them that way and that anyone who says otherwise is somehow wrong. Adulterers and fornicators believe that they are better than homosexuals and that their own trysts, because they're sleeping with the opposite sex, are somehow acceptable in God's sight. It goes on and on like this, with each person deceiving himself into believing that the Bible isn't saying what it says. Satan is in the midst of these debates where people are deceiving themselves, believing one sin is not as detrimental to our spiritual selves as other sins are. This is happening because Satan knows that sin gives us temporary pleasure. It satisfies the flesh. The devil is aware of this because he is sin and the master of it. Satan also knows that if we commit sin, it becomes easier for him to control us.

Here is what the Bible says:

> He that committeth sin is of the devil; for the devil sinneth from the beginning. For this purpose the Son of God was manifested, that he might destroy the works of the devil. Whosoever is born of God doth not commit sin; for his seed remaineth in him: and he cannot sin, because he is born of God. In this the children of God are manifest, and the children of the devil: whosoever doeth not righteousness is not of God, neither he that loveth not his brother. For this is the message that ye heard from the beginning, that we should love one another. (1 John 3:8-11)

Sin is an act of disobedience to God: "Whosoever committeth sin transgresseth also the law: for sin is the transgression of the law" (1 John 3:4). Numerous sins exist—actions we are instructed by God not to engage in. No sin is greater than another. Scripture says, "For whosoever shall keep the whole law, and yet offend in one point, he is guilty of all" (James 2:10). God gave us specific laws to live by, and certain behaviors will jeopardize our eternal souls.

Let us start with the Ten Commandments as given in Exodus 20:3-17:

1. "Thou shalt have no other gods before me."
2. "Thou shalt not make unto thee any graven image...."
3. "Thou shalt not take the name of the LORD thy God in vain...."
4. "Remember the sabbath day, to keep it holy."

5. "Honour thy father and thy mother...."
6. "Thou shalt not kill."
7. "Thou shalt not commit adultery."
8. "Thou shalt not steal."
9. "Thou shalt not bear false witness against thy neighbor."
10. "Thou shalt not covet thy neighbour's house, thou shalt not covet thy neighbour's wife ... nor any thing that is thy neighbour's."

If we engage in breaking any of these, we have committed sin. But it doesn't stop there. We can sin in different ways. We all struggle with certain sins, but sin is sin is sin. It is wrong, and God expects for us to turn away from it. The same message that Jesus gave to the adulterous woman in John 8:11, He speaks to all of us: "Go, and sin no more." No sinner is better off than another sinner. "For he that said, Do not commit adultery, said also, Do not kill. Now if thou commit no adultery, yet if thou kill, thou art become a transgressor of the law" (James 2:11).

When we do not feel sure about what constitutes sin, the best thing to do is consult the Bible. Other people may attempt to lead us astray, especially if they are lovers of the world. In consulting the Bible, though, you will get the whole truth, not just bits and pieces.

Here are a few acts that go against God and entangle many in their destructive webs:

> **Lust:** "But I say unto you, That whosoever looketh on a woman to lust after her hath committed adultery with her already in his heart" (Matt. 5:28).

Anger: "But I say unto you, That whosoever is angry with his brother without a cause shall be in danger of the judgment …" (Matt. 5:22).

Divorce: "But I say unto you, That whosoever shall put away his wife, saving for the cause of fornication, causeth her to commit adultery: and whosoever shall marry her that is divorced committeth adultery" (Matt. 5:32). "Moses because of the hardness of your hearts suffered you to put away your wives: but from the beginning it was not so. And I say unto you, Whosoever shall put away his wife, except it be for fornication, and shall marry another, committeth adultery: and whoso marrieth her which is put away doth commit adultery" (19:8-9). "So then if, while her husband liveth, she be married to another man, she shall be called an adulteress…" (Rom. 7:3).

Evils of the heart: "For out of the heart proceed evil thoughts, murders, adulteries, fornications, thefts, false witness, blasphemies" (Matt. 15:19).

Swearing (i.e., making oaths/vows): "But I say unto you, Swear not at all" (Matt. 5:34). This goes further. We are instructed not to swear by heaven. Also, we are neither to swear "by the earth" nor by our own head (vv. 35-36). We are to let our "yes" and "no" suffice. Anything "more than these cometh of evil" (v. 37).

Judging: "Judge not, that ye be not judged. For with what judgment ye judge, ye shall be judged: and with what measure ye mete, it shall be measured to you again" (Matt. 7:1-2).

Sin is darkness. Living in darkness makes the devil happy. When we live in darkness, we have no hope. No truth can be found there. Eventually people may convince themselves they have resided in darkness for so long that they cannot turn back, and that God will not forgive them. One thing I hear people say that saddens me to the point of tears is, "I know I'm going to hell because I've done too many bad things in my life. I mean, really bad things." People think because they can't forgive themselves, or because the people they've sinned against cannot forgive them, then God will not forgive them either. That is yet another one of the devil's lies. But I beg to differ! According to my Bible:

> All manner of sin and blasphemy shall be forgiven unto men: but the blasphemy against the Holy Ghost shall not be forgiven unto men. And who- soever speaketh a word against the Son of man, it shall be forgiven him: but whosoever speaketh against the Holy Ghost, it shall not be forgiven him, neither in this world, neither in the world to come. (Matt. 12:31-32)

Engaging in sin makes us children of the evil one. Being enwrapped in sin, we walk in darkness and live as agents of the devil. Instead of furthering the kingdom of God, we increase the kingdom of darkness. In denying God's truth we bow down to the god of this world. Satan has been wildly suc- cessful in using his position as the prince of the power of the air to turn us away from God. He knows that many of us are eager to follow what is popular in this world. In going along with the world, we may indeed experience a lot less resistance in our earthly lives. When we are in agreement with the world, we are far less likely to be bashed and called vile names. Going along with the world means that the devil will probably make our paths a little less complicated. But when we go along in this manner, happily rejoicing in our sins and denying the truth, we are playing the role of servant to the devil.

In no way should we hate a person for sinning or choosing to live apart from God. We should always love one another. We should always conduct ourselves in a manner that would make God proud to call us His children. However, we are not to condone sin or to turn a blind eye to it. We are to pray for one another, that each of us will come to the understanding of the truth. We have to uplift one another, not in sin, but in the name of Jesus.

We should not be surprised when the world comes down hard on us, criticizing us for our walk with God. In those times we have to remember that Satan is the god of this world. He is the great deceiver who goes about deceiving the world. He cannot deceive those of us who do not want to be deceived. And, yes, some people want to be deceived, because they would rather believe that living any kind of way they see fit will somehow benefit them and will come with no consequences. I'm convinced that if every person could see the pending consequences for their actions, they would gladly quit living apart from God. There will be consequences for sin, whether we believe it or not. The consequence of sin is eternal suffering. Satan will never tell us that part, though.

3
Satan's Plans

IN THE BEGINNING Satan had a lofty plan. His plan was to be greater than the One who created him. Being in the presence of greatness simply wasn't enough to satisfy the devil. I mean, as an angel in God's kingdom, this Satan fellow had access to everything. But he wanted more. In the heavens he wasn't the head honcho, and he was apparently not happy about that fact. In his heart the devil devised a plan to "ascend above the heights of the clouds" and to "be like the most High" (Isa. 14:14). This was Satan's master plan: to become higher than God.

He failed miserably in his attempt to overtake God, of course. God was—and is—too powerful for him. This could never be one of those cases where the student rises above the teacher. No way, no how! Satan could never overthrow the One who created him in the first place. Not only did Lucifer lose the fight with God, but he was also kicked out of heaven. So he set his sights on more achievable goals. The great deceiver, in his anger, had to devise another plan. In other words his focus changed. He began to set his sights on man, an easier target.

The evil one has a plan for the human race. Being the highly skilled architect that he is, he has drawn up a master plan to help him accomplish the desires of his heart. The devil's plans are clearly spelled out in the Bible: "The thief cometh not, but for to steal, and to kill, and to destroy ..." (John 10:10). The thief's plans are the opposite of God's plans for those who love Him. In the same verse Jesus revealed his plans for us: "... I am come that they might have life, and that they might have it more abundantly." I don't know about you, but I like Jesus's plans for our lives better than the alternative offered by the enemy.

Satan is an avid hunter, roaming around in the earth, preying on us. After he weakens us through sin, he swoops in and devours our souls. We would be mistaken to underestimate his cunning ways. We all have a target on our backs, and the devil's goal is to consume us. Because the devil knows what his end will be, he wants you and me to be sentenced by God to the bottomless pit, and to endure the same suffering as he will. Most of us have probably heard the saying, "Misery loves company." This is one of those cases. Satan is miserable, and he is looking for us to keep him company.

Satan, that old devil, is always searching the earth for the lost and the weak, the ones he feels he can devour. Never forget that we have an enemy whose goal is to trap and to devour those of us who have not taken the time to put on God's armor. Don't think that the devil is simply after people who do not have a relationship with God, though. He also goes after the ones who are seeking to learn about and to know

God. So, just like the persistent evil that pursues us daily, we have to persevere in our efforts to seek God and to do His will.

Remember also that Satan never sleeps. He is always at work, perfecting his plan and looking for opportunities to catch us in our most vulnerable and desperate states. He builds his empire on the backs of all the willing souls who allow themselves to be used by him. Satan's purpose is to hinder us on life's journey, and he uses other people to do it. He did the same thing to Paul when he wanted to visit the church of the Thessalonians. In the First Epistle to the Thessalonians, Paul wrote, "Wherefore we would have come unto you ... but Satan hindered us" (2:18). It is not unheard of for Satan to hinder God's people on their journeys through life, keeping us from loving each other, from doing good to one another, from uniting for the good of all people, from growing closer to God, from learning the truth, and from doing the will of God.

It may be difficult to believe that the devil can wield such tremendous power over believers in Christ. But we know that the father of lies influences our thoughts and actions, and our reactions to and interactions with others. He influences the way the disobedient conduct themselves. He influences their value systems. Some people believe we act the way we do for no reason other than we are either good people or bad people (or a combination of the two). These people don't give Satan credit for his ability to influence our decision-making processes when we fail to include God in everything we do. Because we are beings who take pleasure in things of the flesh, in earthly things, we are more easily open to the devil's influences.

We must remember that Satan is the god of this world and the prince of the power of the air. This means he has the power to influence our thought processes. Because this clever old serpent knows exactly how to ease his way into our minds and into our hearts, we may not even know why we think or act on some of the evil thoughts that cloud our minds. If we hold on to anger and bitterness, these negative emotions give the devil easy access. When we are hell-bent on holding onto sinful thoughts and lusts of the flesh, the devil proudly helps us sink deeper and deeper into a state of madness.

Being crafty, Satan does his research first. He watches us, follows us, and gets to know us before he makes his move. He listens to our conversations, which are oftentimes riddled with gossip, rumors, and untruths. He hears us when we speak negativity, and because he pays close attention to what we say and do, he knows exactly how to push our buttons. The devil usually knows what makes us tick. He will test our faith by throwing every possible negative situation at us. If our faith waivers during these tests, the serpent will ease his way in.

Consider the biblical account of Job. In this book Satan has his eyes on a man who fears God and stands against evil. The devil does his homework on Job. He keeps track of Job's whereabouts and learns what makes Job tick. He doesn't think Job will be faithful to God when he's tested; he believes that Job is faithful only because of what God has blessed him with. That's why Satan targets Job.

So Satan approaches God, along with "the sons of God" at the time they "came to present themselves before the LORD" (1:6), and the Lord asks the devil, "Whence comest thou?" (v. 7). Scripture goes on to say, "Then Satan answered the LORD, and said, From going to and fro in the earth, and from walking up and down in it" (v. 7). God, of course, already knew who the devil had his eyes on: "And the LORD said unto Satan, Hast thou considered my servant Job...?" (v. 8).

Job wasn't doing anything wrong. The scripture says he was an upright man. Satan, remember, will go after anybody—the upright and the sinner alike. Does Satan not seek us out to destroy us even now? The devil is relentless in his pursuit of the human race and his intention to destroy us all. Speaking on behalf of myself, I can say that I am not nearly the righteous man the Bible describes Job as being. I don't come close to being righteous. The sinner in me is very much alive and kicking. If you can say the same about yourself, then you should know that the devil sees you as an easy target. He put Job through some things that would totally destroy a man who doesn't know the power of God to restore him. Everything was taken from Job—his family, his possessions, and his health. But Job knew God, and he knew that God would be able to turn things around in his favor. Job held on and continued to believe in God, even when the devil did everything in his power to try to persuade him that God had forsaken him.

Do you see how the devil picks his prey? He's forever looking for targets. Just picture him in action. Picture a madman bent on destroying everything within his reach. Can you see him? If we don't have the discerning spirit that we receive through fervent prayer, studying the Word of God, being obedient to the Word, and having a personal relationship with God, then we will not recognize Satan until he has accomplished mass destruction in our lives. Do you know anyone who is always running around, destroying everything in their path, spewing their poison, and pitting one person against another by spreading lies? I have known my share of them. These are people being used by Satan to do his dirty work.

Because the devil catches us when we are unaware of his presence, his true identity, or his purpose, he is able to steal from us. *What exactly,* you may be asking yourself, *is that thief called Satan taking from me without my knowledge?* Have you ever found yourself working extra shifts just to make ends meet? Have you ever gotten yourself all wrapped up in survival mode? Does it ever seem as if you have no extra time in your day to meditate on God's Word or to join in fellowship with other believers? Perhaps you are on the run constantly, only to find yourself exhausted at the end of the day, and all you want to do is sleep. But then you are so tired from lack of sleep that you wake up in the morning with very little energy to be as productive as you could, or should, be. You live in a fog. You are irritable, mean, and far from alert.

When our time and our energy have been stolen, we are unable to see the enemy coming. We blindly let him into our lives. It's like opening the door without first asking "Who's there?" Once the devil gets in, it's difficult to get rid of him before he causes a tremendous amount of harm. After Satan steals from us when we are not sober and vigilant, we become bitter from the loss. We are angry that we have to start over. Depending on how much we've lost, we may also feel we are never going to be okay again. We may even feel that life is no longer worth living.

Many times suffering tremendous losses (loss of reputation, material possessions, status, career, etc.) ends with us losing hope and growing continuously more bitter and blaming God for all the bad things that have happened in our lives. We vow to cut ourselves off from God. Some of us turn to alcohol or drugs, or both, as a way to forget the pain of losing something very dear to our hearts. Satan thus steals our health. If no one ever told you that stress steals your health, I am telling you now. Stress weakens the immune system and makes us susceptible to all kinds of diseases. The unholy thief doesn't stop with stealing our health, though.

Satan also wants to steal our minds. He doesn't just rush in and causes us to lose our minds in one stroke. No, he does it a little bit at a time. He makes our lives difficult so we stress ourselves out and fall into depression over things beyond our control—such as injustice and discrimination, being the object of deep-seated hatred, not getting credit for the work we do, being excluded, and being unable to save the world (whatever our definition of saving the world might be). We have to see the devil for exactly who he is: a highly skilled manipulator and the ruler of wickedness. Satan, the thief, is an unmatched expert at his craft. But we play a major role in just how much he is able to steal from us.

When we feel stressed, the devil can steal our hope and make us think we're all alone. I have had times in my own life when I found myself believing that I stood alone. Because so many bad things had already taken place in my life, I expected the worst. I allowed temporary defeat to steal my hope and shake my faith, which was already on low.

When people have been let down and beaten down by life, it's not uncommon for them to give up hope temporarily. What they're doing is losing faith in God. They feel that He has either left them all alone or that He doesn't even exist. Enter the destroyer! The enemy knows exactly when we lose faith and hope, because we've put it out there. We act like hopeless individuals. We tend to say things like, "If there was a God, He wouldn't allow bad things to happen to us." It's that kind of talk that gives the devil access to our lives. He rushes in to convince us that we are indeed all alone in this world and we can't count on anyone but ourselves. When everything we try to accomplish fails, we tend to believe we have nothing and no one.

Hope is having faith in God. Hope is knowing that God has the remedy to all that goes wrong in our lives and walking in the assurance that God has everything under control. God is all we need. Where there is loss of hope, there is loss of meaning and purpose. These losses are followed by a loss of the will to live. Usually what follows is self-destruction.

The enemy also wants to steal our voice. He accomplishes this by presenting us as people who cannot be trusted. The enemy steals our "good" reputation by telling lies and spreading rumors about us. Now a lot can be said about reputation. To some people reputation (or how they appear to the outside world) is of the utmost importance. These people who make the world their god cannot imagine living a life in which they are not held in high esteem in the eyes of public opinion. They have bought into the lie that the people judging them matter more than how they look in God's eyes. The human court of public opinion is made up of people who likely have mastered hiding their skeletons in the closet. The truth is, if we are in good standing with the Lord, our reputation as God-fearing human beings will be enough. A godly life allows us to stand tall, regardless of rumors and gossip. Garnering the praise of men is of little value. Man cannot reward us with a spot in heaven or hell. Yet even with that truth, millions around the world spend their lives striving to be labeled "upstanding" by the court of public opinion. Giving others' opinion of us more credit than we give God is what the great deceiver wants us to do.

When others throw our past in our faces, year after year, our voices tend to grow smaller and more insignificant. The words we have to say soon have no worth because our damaged reputations are bigger than anything we say. When we have been convicted of a crime, for example, fallible men say, "Thanks to his background, he cannot be trusted." In court, if a man has faltered in his life and been caught in wrongdoing, when he gets up to testify, the first thing the opposing attorney says is, "This man has a shady past. He can't be trusted." The members of the jury usually buy into this. So-called Christians even buy into this. Those persons calling out the "shady" past of others act as if they have never lied, cheated, or stolen. It is like they don't think twice about their own imperfections.

This generation sees things the way they want to see them. Everything is based on façades. When worldly people see someone as important—say a police officer, judge, celebrity, wealthy individual, or highly educated person—they somehow can't imagine that person as possibly being imperfect and capable of wrongdoing. Instead the police officer, judge, celebrity, wealthy, or educated person is elevated above "regular" folks, and anything he or she says carries a great deal of weight. He or she is automatically believed. Forget about being poor, being an ex-convict, or both! You are told that your voice has no weight, and the world will scream it loud and clear. In times like these we must remember that Satan is the god of this world, that he was a liar and murderer from the very beginning, and that he clouds the minds of men and women who are separated from God due to their sins. We are up against the devil and his agents, and they are masters of illusions. The devil would love for us to believe we have no hope and that our lives do not matter. Past indiscretions, whether true or not, loom larger than the lives we currently live. Our backgrounds follow us wherever we go. On our path to breaking free of the past that has held us back, we are destined to face one or more of Satan's gatekeepers who will say, "Hey, you can't be trusted with this opportunity because of the blemish on your background." They sit in their seats of judgment and deny our worth. And the sad thing is, millions of people give up without putting up a decent fight. We figure there is no way we could ever make it in a world so unforgiving and cold. This, though, is nothing more than telling ourselves that the enemy is more powerful than God. But, at the same time, the Living Word wants to get a message of hope to us. The Word maintains, "greater is he that is in you, than he that is in the world" (1 John 4:4).

Sometimes we hide ourselves and stay in our place out of fear of rejection and ridicule. Instead of moving on and moving higher and striving for excellence, we remain at the bottom rungs of society, powerless and afraid. I know this from firsthand experience. I've met a great number of people who were there with me, at the bottom—hopeless, powerless, and afraid to climb out of that pit filled with weak people who had given up due to giving too much power to the enemy. During times like these the devil is rejoicing in our failures, because he always celebrates when we are too afraid to walk in the power that God has bestowed upon us.

The great deceiver has fooled the world into believing many lies. Sadly he is accomplishing his goals quite easily! However, once we forge a bond with God and we begin to walk in understanding and wisdom, we start to realize that we are so much more powerful than our background. When we get to know God, we can move beyond our past and live a fulfilling life in the present. Satan is always going to paint a gloomy picture. We must look past the portrait of gloom and doom that the father of lies has painted of our future. He wants nothing more than for us to give up on ourselves and on God. We can take back our voices and make a difference. When we press forward and remember that God can use anybody, regardless of his or her past, we can turn others on to the wonderful power of God. Jesus didn't stop by the local church when He was looking for disciples. He chose sinners like you and me to be His followers. That should kill every lie we have ever been told about how our imperfect pasts will prevent us from accomplishing anything worthwhile.

Satan the thief is also a dream-killer. As children we start out as dreamers, wanting to be this or that. Then we go through some struggles and everything changes. We give up on our dreams when we don't receive the encouragement and positive feedback from those we feel should be there to support us in our endeavors. Many people stop trying when their dreams are dashed. They see themselves as failures and believe the burden of having others see them as failures is not worth continuing the pursuit of that dream. Years might pass, and then they begin to believe they are too old to accomplish their dreams. Giving up means the devil has completed the work he came to do. But dreams do come true when we make God our primary focus.

Satan's ultimate goal is to destroy our souls. He hates that God has prepared a divine place for His children. Satan does not want the place prepared for him; it has no light and is bottomless. He will be bound there for eternity. That is why he wants to keep us in the dark. If he can somehow manage to keep us in the dark, we will become his tenants in hell.

The ruler of darkness uses his children to commit unspeakable sins against humanity, and then he tries to get us to believe that God doesn't exist, because if God were real, bad things wouldn't happen to good people, right? The Bible addresses the subject of "good" people, but I'll save that topic for another chapter. I'll just say here that what man considers "good" is not what God says "good" is. And the devil won't tell us that our defiance of God is the reason we see so much unrest and so many crimes committed against people. The devil won't tell us that our waywardness is why so much evil exists in the world.

It should not amaze believers that the devil is highly successful in separating human beings from God. When I was in the United States Navy, I had a friend who was convinced that God didn't exist. He believed this because, when he was younger—well before he finished school—his mother died. He believed that if God existed, then He would not have taken his mother away from him. My friend shared with me that after his mother died, he couldn't bring himself to believe in God. I was eighteen or nineteen years old at that time and had my own issues with God, so I could offer no words of wisdom to my comrade other than to tell him that I believed in God. At that time believing in God was the extent of my spiritual journey.

My friend wasn't alone in his belief that there is no God. Unbelief in God is prevalent. Today unbelief seems to be the norm. People who were raised to believe in God are now questioning His existence. Many act embarrassed to acknowledge that God exists. They will say things like, "I believe that something is out there" or "I believe in the universe." Or they are quick to say, "I'm not a spiritual person." It is somehow more acceptable to believe one is self-made that to believe that God is the Creator of all things.

We can't see God, so some of us question God's existence or we rationalize that if we can't see Him, then He doesn't exist. That is the devil at work, enticing us with the lie that what we cannot see does not exist! Getting us to believe there is no God puts the prince of this world in the driver's seat. Once in the driver's seat, Satan is able to lead us any which way he chooses.

The thief's end is near. He's angry, and he's out to claim us as his own by any means necessary. His success rate is high. Sin remains an appetizing dish to the vast majority of us. It satisfies our hungry flesh. Iniquity is presented to us with a sweet-smelling aroma that lures us in. Yet it is a death trap. Sin is the devil's way of making us one of his own. Our engaging in sin is entertainment to the devil. When we defy God, we become slaves to the devil. We make him our father, and his lies become our lies.

Satan's plan for us is our destruction. But God's plan for us is life eternal. God is rooting for us. That is why He sent His Son Jesus to save us, because God's mercy is abundant and everlasting: "For God sent not his Son into the world to condemn the world; but that the world through him might be saved" (John 3:17). To further state Jesus's purpose, we only have to look at 1 Timothy 1:15: "Christ Jesus came into the world to save sinners." It is not God who wants to harm us or to send us to live an eternity in the pit of hell, where we would know suffering and lack as we have never known it before. Satan seeks to devour us. God wants to save us from Satan.

4

The Destroyer Is in the Headlines

HAVE YOU EVER heard the saying, "The devil is in the details"? Those who trust in their own wisdom seem to believe that Satan has nothing at all to do with the evil in our world. Those people are quick to say, "Stop blaming the devil and take responsibility for your own actions." This statement is based on their belief that no force in the world entices or tempts or influences people to do evil. They may also say, "The devil has nothing to do with the evil that people choose to do." That statement is simply not true.

Of course people must take responsibility for their actions and stop blaming others for the evil they choose to do. They, and the people who love them, should also stop trying to blame what goes wrong in their lives on some kind of medical ailment, a bad upbringing, "the system," or hanging with a "bad" crowd. I'm sure you can't even count the number of times you've heard people blame the wrong their loved ones do on "hanging with the wrong crowd." But when bad things happen, it has a lot to do with how the devil uses spiritual wickedness to influence the willing participant.

An evil force is at work in the world, going about deceiving millions of people and persuading them to do terrible things to themselves and to their neighbors. Putting all the blame on people is easier, because in reality a number of people believe only in what they can see, no matter how many times they read that we fight against the rulers of darkness. Self-proclaimed Christians also fall for the devil's trick and begin to doubt God, because they are desperate to see some physical sign that God exists. It is something about the physical that excites man to belief. So they search high and low for physical signs and are led away into the realm of darkness. We cannot see the spiritual wickedness in the world without being connected to the Divine One. Satan is not featured in pictures that circulate around the Internet or in magazines or newspapers. You've probably seen the photos of clouds that are shaped in the image of angels and/or demons. That is a trick of the devil. It is not a physical war.

Getting upset at people for their evil does nothing to stop the devil and his camp from being so successful in claiming victory in their lives and causing grief in the lives of those who have been victimized. Our battle is not against flesh and blood, but rather is a spiritual war (Eph. 6:12), and thus we should not fight the same way as the world does. The Bible maintains, "For the weapons of our warfare are not carnal, but mighty through God to the pulling down of strong holds" (2 Cor. 10:4). These strongholds are anything that keeps us from advancing forward in the name of Jesus. In order to defeat evil and to overcome strongholds, we have to call on God and ask Him to fight our battles.

Satan and his angels have caused the world to fall into a spiritual war. They continually work to hinder us, to oppress us, and to bring harm to us. We may find ourselves on the losing end of spiritual battles due to our own foolish "wisdom." That is, we think we are fighting against man, when in actuality we are fighting against the rulers of the darkness. We are fighting wars that cannot be won using man's own wisdom. The following "wars" can only be won through love, prayer, fasting, and righteous living:

> The war on drugs
> The war on gang violence
> The war on racism and discrimination
> The war on hatred
> The war on inequality
> The war on suicide and homicide
> The war on poverty, homelessness, and hunger
> The war on disease
> The war on police brutality
> The war on domestic and international terrorism

It's easy to give something a label and then use that label to explain away the ills of society. That's what we do as human beings. We believe our own hype. We feel we have all the answers. We are sure that if everyone would do as we say, the world would be a much better place. Unless our answer is God, though, our problems will never end and the battles we face will never be won. God is the answer. And if you didn't hear me the first time, God is the answer.

The devil spearheads every attack against humanity. We are in the final stretch of this earthly war, and the devil's work is growing increasingly more devastating by the day. He is making significant progress. As long as we believe the devil to be nothing more than a figment of our imagination, the numbers on his scoreboard will rise and people will walk around dumbfounded because they cannot explain the devastation of the world in human terms. Their ignorance or rejection of holy truth leaves them in a state of bewilderment. Something is going on, and they simply cannot figure it out. The devil just smiles and continues to build his empire, using none other than those of us who reject God's wisdom.

Today's headlines read like the "Who's Who among Satan's Chosen." The people who make up the world, as it is today, make the father of death extremely happy. He must be sitting back and laughing at how little effort he's having to put forth to destroy mankind. Acts of evil have become more widespread than acts of kindness. As a matter of fact, when we show kindness and concern for our neighbors, many think it's strange. Some folks—with hidden agendas themselves—think an ulterior motive lies behind our random acts of kindness. Because malice or deceit is their motive, some people are automatically skeptical of any person who shows kindness and goodwill to others. The wicked expect everyone to be like them. But the devil's lies should not prevent us from showering others with kindness. "And let us not be weary in well doing: for in due season we shall reap, if we faint not" (Gal. 6:9). The accusatory tactics used by the wicked should not put out the believers' fire to do good. Their accusations and deceit should come as no surprise; neither should they keep us from being missionaries of Christ.

Spiritual wickedness keeps the lovers of this world in the dark and fighting against others and killing each other. Still, we see the devil in others, but not in ourselves. What we do not see is that Satan wants to use all of us. All our hands have been dirty. Some of us, though, have chosen to wash our hands and to treat people like we want to be treated, whereas others have decided there is nothing wrong with mistreating their neighbor. Wickedness thrives in this world. The reason being, people do not believe they will have to answer to a higher power!

Let me say this again: the devil is here. He's successfully recruiting soldiers to fight in his army. The devil and his recruits go about setting traps. They enjoy every second of their hunt. We have only to open our spiritual eyes to see that believers are their targets. The enemy is not worried about persons who do not believe in God and His Word. Satan's already claimed those individuals as his own. However, if we believers are to avoid the traps of the wicked, we have to allow God to be our guide. God will reveal Satan and his angels' whereabouts to us and prevent us from falling into their snares. Hopefully we will not slip into a sinful lifestyle, but in the event that we backslide and find ourselves subjects in Satan's headlines, we can still turn to God and seek redemption before it is too late.

The headlines reveal the destroyer's whereabouts to the true followers of Christ. They tell us what the devil is up to on a minute-by-minute basis. Look at all the horrible ills infecting societies all around the world: war, murder, suicide, kidnapping, rape, robbery, arson, terrorism (domestic and foreign), vigilantism, and the latest derogatory comment or hate speech! You name it, it's taking place as you read this passage. It's no great wonder why unbelievers are always so anxious, fearful, and paranoid. Without a secure relationship with God, they have nothing to keep them in perfect peace. They fall off the edge of the mental cliff and they have no idea why they've fallen. They're crushed by life and the harsh realities that present themselves without interruption. Without God being our source of protection, evil prevails.

One devastating occurrence that keeps popping up in the media is the mass murder of innocent people—innocent not in the sense that they have done nothing wrong, but innocent in the sense that they were minding their own business, and some person who has allowed the devil to enter into the recesses of his heart came in and took the lives of people who were no physical threat to the murderer nor to the lives of others. The world's chorus sings, "He is guilty and death was necessary." The devil could not have made a more evil statement.

The lost of the world cheer on the murderers and the liars who hold positions of authority. Spiritual wickedness in high places wins out in a world filled with lost souls. Minds are blinded. However, the minds of believers know that to kill and to lie are sins against God. An individual can lie about the ugliness inside his heart and have the world believe him, but God knows all, and He is the One who matters. The spiritually wicked who hold high positions are not untouchable. They may escape the biased hand of justice here on earth, but the wicked will never truly escape. They will be held accountable for their actions.

The devil and his angels, through spiritual wickedness, handpick earthly bodies to carry out murderous attacks on unsuspecting victims. Then they use a slew of excuses, most of which are accepted, and the supposed investigations turn out in favor of the wicked ones, who successfully work in cahoots with their wicked comrades. We live in a time when evil behavior is rewarded. The Bible lets us know that the world (those not doing the will of God) loves its own (John 15:19). It should not seem strange, then, that a murderer is let off the hook and given a pat on the back and some financial support for taking the life of a "lesser" human being.

Many of the events in the world today, I could not make up if I tried. Criminal activity is playing out like a number one box-office thriller, except it is real. God's commandments are being broken at will. Evil is showing its true face and breathing fiery darts with rapid speed. The vigilante, the thief, the liar, the oppressor, and the wolf hiding in sheep's clothing are destroying lives and laughing about it. The reason evil has such a high success rate is that armies of believers fear the enemy more than they believe in God! Fearful believers fear what they may lose if they stand up to wickedness. Little do they know, the fearful, just like the unbelieving, will have no place in God's kingdom. Their belief in God, if they die cowards, will be in vain.

The battle against darkness will continue until Jesus returns. It is a cold, hard fact. It is biblical. Yet believers and nonbelievers alike are trying to fight evil with evil, and it simply will not work. Fighting evil with evil only begets more evil. It is a never-ending cycle of nothingness. Doesn't anybody see that using ungodly tactics in the fight against demonic spirits plays right into the hands of the wicked? We cannot defeat evil with evil or use anger to defeat anger. No one can use the prince of this world's weapons against him. Satan and his angels are masters at what they do. To thwart their fiery darts, we are going to have to join together in boldness, love, and truth. To wield power against the evil one, we must first turn away from sin. Then we must unleash God on every demonic situation that threatens to destroy us and our families. We have no other recourse against the evil one. God is it! We must make God our friend and not the world.

We should never mistake the world as a friend. The world is not a friend to the believer, but a lover of the unbeliever. The world, filled with more nonbelievers than believers, is joined together against God and His people. Evildoers stick together in their mischief and are able to win. Those who know God but choose not to call on Him to defeat the enemy will suffer defeat. Evil can only be defeated by declaring the blood of Jesus over it.

Evil lurks inside all of us. No one is excluded. We label one another "good" or "bad" or "both good and bad." Have you ever heard someone refer to another by saying, "There is not a bad bone in his body"? The Bible, though, describes the true nature of man's heart. The Good Book describes man's heart as such: "the imagination of man's heart is evil from his youth" (Gen. 8:21). That's probably hard for us to read, since some of us believe that we are model citizens with "good" hearts. But if God said it, that's how it is. It is a hard-hitting statement of truth. And it is the only truth I will ever believe. How about you?

Every evil imaginable resides in the heart of man, even from his youth. Can you imagine that? Whether or not we can visualize the evil that lurks in the hearts of men, women, and children, it is there, suppressed in some and realized in others. If you don't believe this, take a look at the young people who have committed every crime possible, from petty theft to cold-blooded murder. Where does it come from? It comes from wickedness that enters into the hearts of every man, woman, and child. It comes from parents not aligning their children with God and His Word. It comes from not training a child in the ways of God. The Bible gives perfect instruction: "Train up a child in the way he should go: and when he is old, he will not depart from it" (Prov. 22:6). Evil comes from our infatuation with sin. Growing to love sin, we grow to hate God's instructions. This is the reason the world continues to sink lower and lower.

The lovers of the world have their own belief systems, and they do not include God. Man considers himself rational and explains the problems we face in terms of his own knowledge. Man's foolish wisdom has reached dangerous heights. "For the wisdom of this world is foolishness with God. For it is written, He taketh the wise in their own craftiness" (1 Cor. 3:19). Every time a man thinks his word is gospel, God steps in and shows him the errors of his ways by allowing to happen the very thing man said would not happen. When man's wisdom fails him, he is dumbfounded, but he will almost never admit that his wisdom is foolishness. Man doesn't have to admit his thoughts are vain, because "The Lord knoweth the thoughts of the wise, that they are vain" (1 Cor. 3:20). However, man's belief that he alone is capable of fixing this broken world will keep it in ruins and also keep people running amuck, destroying and being destroyed.

Speaking of destruction, this generation is both witnessing it and participating in it. Young people are ever the clever ones. With the help of man's vain wisdom, young people have wrestled power away from the adults. Yet the shutters hanging over the spiritual eyes of man prevent him from seeing this. This generation of young people knows they have the power, so they run with it. They run into their own destruction and also that of their unbelieving parents and the other unbelieving adults who operate outside the wisdom of God.

This destruction leaves the "professionals" confused. They assume that the child must have had a traumatic upbringing. Or they believe some medical explanation must exist for the youth contributing to societal ills. The answer to all our problems and all societal ills is and will always be biblical. I'd say, based on what the Bible teaches, that God has been left out of the equation, and without God we can do nothing and solve nothing. We can study behavioral science or any other field until the end of time, but if we do not base our lives upon God's Word, we will always be proven wrong.

Our wrongs bring about suffering. We forsake God by going against His teachings, then we wonder where God is when everything in our lives begins to make no sense. Worse, we twist it and make God out to be responsible for our suffering. Getting us to blame God for our problems is a tactic of the devil. God does not forsake us. We forsake Him by choosing to do the very things He instructs us not to do. He is not the reason for the bad things that happen in the world. We are to blame—and, of course, the devil. We are following in the footsteps of the world and the devil instead of in the footsteps of Jesus. That is the real problem.

People are succumbing to their inner and outer demons. Inner demons are those lingering in our own heads, making us feel inadequate, useless, "less than," depressed, alone, lost, and a deep sense of self-hatred. The outer demons are the people in our lives who hinder us. Outer demons are also our sinful behaviors, which tear away at our souls. Both sets of demons contribute to the negative headlines we read about, the ones that detail man's tragic fall.

The headlines are saturated with stories of the decline of humanity. Have you read the headlines lately? Tuned in to

the news on TV? Listened to or observed the glorifying of
sexual immorality, material wealth, hate speech, witchcraft,
strife, lies, and various other sins in the world? People are killing each other for sport. So-called civilized societies are pro-
moting discrimination and hiding racist behaviors with a lying
tongue. The rich oppress the poor. The poor are in constant
conflict with each other, taking out their frustrations on one
another. A continuous, vicious cycle of conflict, turmoil, and
chaos will never see the end of day until Jesus returns. Evil
will continue its downpour of torrential rains. The believer,
if he is to overcome the world, must shun such behavior and
seek God without ceasing. As tempting as it might be to participate in the craziness being glorified in the world, we must
stand strong in the Lord.

People are doing just about anything to get attention,
and they don't care if the attention is positive or negative.
The more negative the act, the more attention it draws. Satan
loves it. Social media prove that people will do just about
anything to get their fifteen minutes of fame, which almost
always includes ditching God and riding with the devil. The
souls desperate for attention will lie, cry, argue, fight, and
risk their lives and the lives of others for personal gain. The
more the devil's gig pays, the lower the lost soul will go. These
people's minds have been blinded by the devil, and they show
how void of the truth they are by crediting God for their "success." When we are successful in acting sinfully, Satan is the
one who has bestowed that "blessing" upon us. God has nothing to do with crude, rude, and lewd behavior.

It's been said and must be said again that man's heart
imagines evil day in and day out. I'm not proud of it, but
my heart has imagined evil and continues to do so. Being a

believer does not exclude me from having thoughts of evil. Anytime we think ill of people, anytime we wish someone anything other than the best, anytime we lust after people or things or are envious of others, we are imagining evil. It's the flesh. Dying to the flesh is an everyday process. It is the willingness to die to the flesh that prevents us from acting out our evil thoughts. Sacrificing the flesh prevents spiritual wickedness from taking over our lives. If anyone tells us he or she has never had impure or evil thoughts, or has never felt something other than love in their hearts, they are liars. Run! They are fooling themselves. People in denial leave an opening for the devil to come in and use them. They will be the ones most likely to make the headlines for carrying out the devil's plans.

Headlines spell out a wide range of man's evil as influenced by Satan. It can't be ignored, nor should it be. People are jumping to their deaths, pulling the trigger on themselves, and walking into churches, schools and workplaces and blowing away their neighbors, peers and coworkers. The perpetrators of scams destroy countless families—their own families and others' as well. Victims are left in financial ruin. The victims didn't see the fraud or the consequences coming until most or all of their finances were lost. Because of man's disobedience, he is having a difficult time understanding what is really going on.

The unbeliever naturally has some confusion about what evil looks like. But for believers, reading the Bible, keeping our minds on the Creator, and praying for a discernible spirit are keys to keeping our feet planted on solid ground. When the world is running around in circles and people are losing their minds and being caught in webs of deception, those of us who stand firmly on God's truth will not faint, nor will we fall apart because of fear. Evil will not ruin our lives, because the world is not our focus.

We need to constantly remind ourselves—whether we are having the time of our lives or we are suffering the pain of defeat—that the God in us is greater than the god of this world. God resides in the believer who keeps His Word. Satan resides in the world and is of the world. He has nothing to do with God. He is a liar! He will attempt to hinder us in our daily walk. When the Word of God abides in us, we are able to distinguish between the Spirit of God and the spirit of the wicked one. Our actions should make God proud.

> Love not the world, neither the things that are in the world. If any man love the world, the love of the Father is not in him. For all that is in the world, the lust of the flesh, and the lust of the eyes, and the pride of life, is not of the Father, but is of the world. (1 John 2:15-16)

The world offers misery in abundance. It sweeps us in, tempting us with things, with fame and fortune and popularity, with social media "friends," and with the best seats in the house. It applauds our accomplishments and makes us feel wanted and accepted. The world lays out the red carpet and throws us fancy parties. We are reeled in by the praise of the world. Then the world suddenly pulls the carpet out from under our feet and leaves us confused and broken. The world moves on, enticing someone else, and we are left wondering what happened. We try to recapture the glory days, but they are no more. We are lost, overwhelmed by sadness and bitterness. Some of us never recover. Because we have lived for the world for so long, we remain caught up and lost in a whirlwind of confusion. We cannot simply walk away from the world that once showed us so much love and support. In our confusion we walk around trying to prove to the world that we belong, that we are somebody. Our relationship with the world has us caught up in a fog and God never enters our thoughts. The world is our god, and it is one cold place.

Those of us who have ears, let us hear: God is the only way! He can offer peace beyond what we are able to comprehend (Phil. 4:7). And that peace is not temporary. We don't have to be a headline that glorifies Satan. Everything the world has to offer is short-term. That includes a false sense of security. As long as we are in love with this wicked world, we will become well acquainted with disappointment. Being a friend of the world means being an enemy of God. Here is what James had to say concerning our relationship with the world: "Ye adulterers and adulteresses, know ye not that the friendship of the world is enmity with God? whosoever therefore will be a friend of the world is the enemy of God" (4:4). We have to choose between being a friend of the world or making God the most important being in our lives. We cannot do both. It is impossible.

5
Man's Justice

ISAIAH 30:18 STATES, "The Lord is a God of judgment."
He loves justice and hates injustice. Therefore, "God will not
do wickedly, neither will the Almighty pervert judgment" (Job
34:12). Justice, according to man, is blind. When we think of
justice, we may picture a statue of Lady Justice blindfolded
and holding balance scales in her left hand. The idea is that
justice is balanced and that it treats everybody fairly and
equally, and that no outside influences come into play, such
as someone's socioeconomic status, position, race, or education. But, like man, justice is flawed. Man's justice is lacking
and imperfect, and it often favors certain people over others.

It would be great if justice was truly blind and if people
standing before the judgment seat always received equal
treatment. The fact is, not everyone is considered equal in the
eyes of the court. The judge, jury member, attorney, detective, and other law enforcement officials bring with them
biases and prejudices, and are incapable of rendering true
justice. The justice system comprises many men and women
who have no regard for equal "justice for all." According to

the Living Word, "None calleth for justice, nor any pleadeth for truth: they trust in vanity, and speak lies; they conceive mischief, and bring forth iniquity" (Isa. 59:4).

The scales of justice are unbalanced. Our current criminal justice system is a perfect example of just how flawed man's justice is. It's off, way off. If all people were treated equally under the law, the prison population would closely resemble the nation's population. Individuals the system considers "redeemable" are shown much mercy. Others are considered animals and shown no mercy at all. This separation of the "redeemable" from the "animal" is based solely on man's respect of persons. The keeper of justice decides who deserves a second and third chance. Often the justice system takes into consideration a person's physical characteristics, education level (and even the school attended), standing in the community, family background, etc.

How can the law, written by man whose thoughts are continually evil, be grounded in the concept of justice for all? It cannot. How can man, who is biased and self-serving, mete out justice to all men equally? He cannot. The law is unjust today. The law was unjust yesterday. The law will be unjust tomorrow. The handing out of "justice" will remain flawed as long as man is running the system. The sins of man prevent him from upholding the law fairly for all people. Justice and a sinful nature do not see eye to eye. "Justice," sadly, comes wrapped in different packages for different people.

The bad news about injustice: it isn't going anywhere. Authorities handing down sentences will continue to rule as they see fit, apart from God. The agents of the law will choose whom to save and whom to condemn based on the inner workings of their hearts. Remember this scripture concerning the heart of man: "The heart is deceitful above all things, and desperately wicked: who can know it?" (Jer. 17:9). A person can possess a good heart only if God gives him a new heart, meaning if we do not abide in God and ask Him to create in us a new heart, then our hearts will remain wicked. God says, "A new heart also will I give you, and a new spirit will I put within you: and I will take away the stony heart out of your flesh, and I will give you an heart of flesh" (Ezek. 36:26). Man rules with an unjust heart, and it perverts justice. In man's heart is no mercy. However, God can change the impure and merciless heart, if we would only ask.

Justice here on earth is discriminatory. We often witness it and complain, wondering why some people get probation while others are handed significant prison time for the same crime, even though they have similar criminal histories. The truth is, justice is different, depending on how one is viewed in the eyes of the imperfect individual who sits upon the bench of judgment—the one handing out what he considers to be justice. So justice has eyes that see what it wants to see, but refuses to look in the mirror at the out-of-control monster staring back at it. Its eyes are open to one's ethnic background, social and economic status, family background, level of education, position/career, celebrity and fame, lifestyle, whom the person knows, and other factors. Again: justice is not blind.

The rich do not receive the same punishment as the poor or even those living with average means. Leniency and mercy are showered upon the rich and famous almost endlessly. You don't believe me? I invite you to take a look at the sentences they receive and compare them with what the "average joe" gets. The rich get one break after another. For their crimes they get a tap on the wrist and an abundance of mercy from the courts. Justice for the rich and famous offers hope. They are not crushed. They find favor because of their money, the testimony of their many friends, the lawyers who argue their cases, the judges who hold them in high esteem, the jury who sees them as deserving or innocent just because of what they have and who they are. In the system of so-called blind justice, the rich and famous are relieved of their burdens, while the poor are crushed and considered guilty before they are given the opportunity to argue their case. Justice goes something like this: *"If you can't pay for the best defense, you lose."*

In this age a poor person is rarely considered innocent. Lawyers sell out the poor without blinking an eye, but represent the rich with a mighty hand. The house of justice is filled with corruption. Its members are motivated by personal gain. It is a house where deals are made and where bribes exchange hands. Hands are shaken among the wicked. Some judges have TV shows and will do anything for fame and fortune. They readily crush plaintiffs and defendants with tongues of death. They consider themselves civil, educated, and upstanding, yet they act like thugs and criminals. These are the people who make up the house of justice. We are supposed to believe these same people hand out justice properly and equitably.

The devil chooses the disconnected to help spread the lie that we live in a just society. To get this lie believed by the majority, Satan grants mercy to them, and because he shows them mercy, he is able to trick them into believing the law is just. If a person is not pursued and unjustly profiled by the law or does not have a history of bad experiences with the law, he will tend to believe the law is just. Therefore he is blinded to the injustices faced by others. That is how cunning the devil is. The house of justice keeps the lie going in an effort to paint its system in a positive light. Because it is successful in spreading the lie and convincing the world's population that the system is not broken, oppression and injustice continue to make for big business. People in love with the world are disconnected from the truth. However, the worldly give ear to what the world says. What does the Bible say about worldly people? It says, "They are of the world: therefore speak they of the world, and the world heareth them" (1 John 4:5).

A person's background plays a large part in obstructing justice and withholding mercy. More often than not, an individual with a felony on his record is seen as "damaged goods." Not many people will say that aloud, but they don't have to. Actions speak louder than words. A person with a troubled background has difficulty getting a job that pays a livable wage. He cannot obtain housing, qualify for certain federal aid, or take advantage of certain opportunities. Individuals with criminal backgrounds are all but cast away to an isolated island of doom. Doors close in their faces quicker than they can reach for the handle. They are given little chance, as their backgrounds overshadow them and follow them wherever they go.

World systems are in place to kill any hope of survival for the oppressed. A lifetime of punishment is what felons face. There is no such thing as a fair chance once a man has paid the price for his crimes. Let's not forget about the numerous innocent men and women who have been convicted of crimes they did not commit, or forced to confess to crimes they knew nothing about. Some of these people are now being released after serving many years of their lives in prison. The "offenders" of justice—holding such positions as district attorney, defense attorney, investigator, lead detective, and judge—almost never admit to their wrongs and will deny with a stone-cold heart that justice was perverted. In many cases the statute of limitations passes, and no form of financial assistance is offered to those who suffered miscarriages of justice.

"Flawed" sums up the earthly house of justice. It is a place where, oftentimes, innocent men are found guilty and guilty men go free. Man's system of justice is operated by self-righteous, unforgiving, and unmerciful men. It destroys men's souls. It is a system that thrives in darkness, operates in darkness, and is kept in place by darkness. Agents of the devil use a person's background to either discredit him or to glorify and praise him. In court and in the world, a man is identified by the blemishes on his record. By those blemishes he is labeled a liar, a bad apple, and someone who can't be trusted. Never mind the reality that we have all done wrong! Never mind if that blemish was caused by a lie. A person's background can make him susceptible to ongoing injustice, because he is going to be seen as someone who is prone to criminal behavior. Injustice cannot see the whole human being and does not understand that we are all flawed. It is incapable of issuing second chances. But thank God for His justice!

True justice is blind. It doesn't see race. It has no regard for a person's position or standing in the community. It cares not where a person was born, what his family name is, where he went to school, how many degrees he holds, or what his net worth is. True justice doesn't care if you are an "average joe" or a man in uniform. If you commit a crime, true justice will let you know you are wrong. True justice doesn't pick and choose whom it will punish. It holds everyone accountable while at the same time offering mercy. True justice views every human being as equal, and its sentences reflect that truth.

But on earth no true justice exists. The only true justice will appear when we all face the Throne of Judgment. There will be no hiding from God. We will be judged with no respect of status. "For there is no respect of persons with God" (Rom. 2:11). This is how true justice is going to play out:

> ... the dead, small and great, stand before God; and the books were opened: and another book was opened, which is the book of life: and the dead were judged out of those things which were written in the books, according to their works. And the sea gave up the dead which were in it; and death and hell delivered up the dead which were in them: and they were judged every man according to their works. (Rev. 20:12-13)

God is the ultimate judge. Darkness cannot hide from God. Injustice may be rampant in the world, but we must not be overwhelmed. We must not believe that evildoers are getting away with their crimes. The wicked will pay a steep price for oppressing the poor and turning a blind eye to injustice. God says, "My righteousness is near; my salvation is gone forth, and mine arms shall judge the people" (Isa. 51:5).

In the day of the prophet Jeremiah, God instructed Jeremiah to deliver a message "to the house of the king of Judah" (Jer. 22:1). God had already laid down the law that the people were to follow, but disobedience persisted. The Lord said, "Execute ye judgment and righteousness" (v. 3). The prophet Isaiah also delivered a strong message from the

Lord: "Learn to do well; seek judgment, relieve the oppressed, judge the fatherless, plead for the widow" (Isa. 1:17). God is serious about justice and the house of justice doing right by men. To those who are tasked with handing out justice in this age, God is speaking those same words. Still, the perverting of justice goes on. The house of justice will have to pay a price for its disobedience. God says, "But if ye will not hear these words, I swear by myself, saith the LORD, that this house shall become a desolation" (Jer. 22:5).

While injustice will always be with us, there is good news: "God is our refuge and strength, a very present help in trouble" (Ps. 46:1). The trouble is, injustice still exists. The answer to that trouble is, a just God is waiting to help us. God says, "I will uphold thee with the right hand of my righteousness" (Isa. 41:10). I don't know about you, but those words are all the comfort I need to know that injustice will never again have power over my life.

People are running around in vain, trying to figure out how to put an end to the injustices swallowing up the helpless and the hopeless. They are looking for answers, wanting to know why innocent people are being gunned down by the very people who are sworn to protect and serve them, and why murderers are walking away, being left to kill again. Their search is in vain, because not very many people are looking for the solution in the scriptures. And in the scriptures is where the answer lies. Instead men are taking matters into their own hands, becoming murderers themselves. Not only are they becoming murderers, but they are spreading blasphemous statements about God, saying there is no God. They say, in their anger and ignorance, that the only justice "we" are going to receive is the justice we hand out ourselves. The

Living Word teaches, "Blessed are all they that wait for him" (Isa. 30:18). God will handle the poison that is injustice—if we live for Him, trust in Him, and wait on Him. God sees and God knows. Justice will be served by the King of Justice.

6
Hate and Division

HATE AND DIVISION go hand in hand. Hate causes division. Where hate is, division resides. Just like you and I were born to an earthly mother and father, so was the spirit of hate. Hate is born of Satan. Hate is a demonic spirit that leads to total destruction. It is a spirit prevalent in the world today. Because of it societies are divided. Hate is a hardening of the heart. It corrodes the mind. A man is the makeup of his heart, "for as he thinketh in his heart, so is he" (Prov. 23:7). The hateful heart is a disease to the soul. And the soul diseased with hate is a soul that belongs to the destroyer called Satan.

It is no secret that we are living in a time when hate abounds. Hate runs wild everywhere, both nearby and in distant lands. Hate is a dish served in abundance and with seeming pleasure. Hate-mongers have come out in the open, with those deadly vipers boldly forsaking their hiding places in the midst of uncut grass. Serpents are revealing themselves, and their leader, the devil, couldn't be more proud. But let us not be fooled. To accomplish their destructive goals, many are remaining in hiding, being in positions of power and influence.

They are going after the sinner and the just. The sinner, who is more susceptible, will prove to be an easier target, for they can't see the devil coming. Hate will prove more destructive in the life of the sinner. The just have to continue on their path, taking care not to allow the father of hate into their hearts, because hate is in full force and moving along at lightning speed. Whoever is caught living outside God's protection will be trampled.

Those on the side of evil will use every tactic they can to attack anyone who speaks out against hate. They will engage in name-calling, manipulation, lies, and whatever tactic they have to use to deny that hatred is hatred. For that reason it is important to have a spirit of discernment. Usually a fool is discovered when he opens his mouth to speak, because "a fool's voice is known by multitude of words" (Eccles. 5:3). The hate-filled person will eventually slander the people he hates. The devil's agents will be there to back him, as the hate-monger usually has a large following. Have we not seen our share of this lately, where hatred is nurtured and defended by the followers of it?

It may or may not be a surprise to you that the first on the list to be hated is God, the Creator of all that is. Jesus reported, "If the world hate you, ye know that it hated me before it hated you (John 15:18). Not only was Jesus hated before we were hated, He said, "They hated me without a cause" (v. 25). Those scriptures, hidden in our hearts, will keep us from being surprised every time one of the liar's earthly angels hurl hate-filled insults at us. God, the One who gives us life and showers us with love, has always faced hatred and so that puts us humans who find ourselves the targets of hate in excellent company. Also, knowing that God is hated and hated without a cause should lessen the effectiveness of the demonic actions of people when we find ourselves in similar situations. We should be honored to experience something that God Himself has experienced.

"If a man say, I love God, and hateth his brother, he is a liar: for he that loveth not his brother whom he hath seen, how can he love God whom he hath not seen?" (1 John 4:20). No one on earth can love God and hate another human being. It is biblically impossible. A lifetime of lies will not hide that truth. Whoever hates his neighbor is a child of the ruler of the bottomless pit. "He that saith he is in the light, and hateth his brother, is in darkness even until now" (2:9). If we ever have an occasion when we are faced with hate, know that the person who hates is blind and is not aware that he is blind. "But he that hateth his brother is in darkness, and walketh in darkness, and knoweth not wither he goeth, because that darkness hath blinded his eyes" (v. 11). Every single person on the face of the earth who allows hate to rule his life is blind. His heart is a cold stone into which no good enters or exits.

When hate says, "I love God," the spiritually connected put themselves in a position to be able to see past lies and deceit and are not caught off guard. In other words hate can yell from a mountaintop that it is love, but the children of God will not be tricked into believing the lie or be destroyed by it. The Bible instructs us to "not love in word, neither in tongue; but in deed and in truth" (3:18). It is not enough to say we love another. God insists that we show our love by doing right by our brothers and sisters, treating them with kindness.

"Whosoever hateth his brother is a murderer: and ye know that no murderer hath eternal life abiding in him" (v. 15). Two pieces of information are given in this scripture: if you hate another human being, you are a murderer; and a murderer has no eternal life. People who hate are murders who belong to their father the devil. Hate equals murder. The two are the same.

Hate elevates paranoia, and then the hater, with his head full of poisonous thoughts, embarks upon a murderous journey, causing division and recruiting like-minded murderers along the way. They cover one another in their wickedness and walk away heroes in the eyes of their followers and supporters. Their support is far from lacking. Neither is God's support for those who are doing His will.

God reminds us that it is not He who gives us the spirit of hate, but Satan, who so effortlessly persuades us that it is okay to hate and that we are justified in our hatred of others. Some hate groups have the audacity to use scripture to make their case. They travel the world, spreading messages of hate and division. They attend rallies and they march, holding signs that bear hateful scribblings, telling people how much God hates them—yes, hates the person, when God loves the person and hates the sin. As we have seen, scripture calls these people blind. Hate groups have always existed and convinced themselves that they are doing the work of God. They eagerly plant the seed of hate and division. This is the spirit of hate, whose origin is in darkness. The truth is that God has given his children the spirit of love (2 Tim. 1:7). Don't be deceived!

Hatred escorted Jesus to the cross. Hate falsely labeled him a "malefactor" (John 18:30). It was hatred that screamed for Jesus, who is love, to be hanged and then delivered Him into the hands of Pilate—delivered up by His own people. Pilate asked Jesus, "Thine own nation and the chief priests have delivered thee unto me: what hast thou done?" (v. 35).

What had Jesus done? He fed the poor, healed the sick, raised the dead, spread the gospel of truth, led people out of darkness, befriended the outcast, and loved everyone. That was the problem. Sinners wanted to remain lost, and Jesus was bringing light to dark places. He had to be done away with. He was a threat to a wicked world. The spiritually sick person does not need a reason to hate his neighbor. All he needs is for you to walk in truth, and he will call for you to be crucified.

Can you imagine the amount of hate it must have taken for people to falsely accuse Jesus—to arrest, try, and convict Him for being who He said He was? The Jews addressed Pilate concerning what should be done with Jesus: "We have a law, and by our law he ought to die, because he made himself the Son of God" (19:7). Have you ever pleaded your innocence with the enemy only to hear him label you a liar and pronounce you guilty of an offense you did not commit? If your answer is "yes," you have tasted a small portion of the suffering Jesus tasted. Pilate said to the chief priests and officers, "Take ye him, and crucify him: for I find no fault in him" (v. 6). Pilate found no fault in Jesus, yet he did not fight to save Him. To satisfy a deceived people, Pilate turned Jesus over into the hands of murderers. Talk about an injustice! They made Jesus out to be a liar. How much more will the agents of the father of lies accuse us?

Being a friend of Jesus means being an enemy to the world. Being an enemy to the world often makes us targets of lies, rumors, and gossip. Or those who have no doubt of our innocence will hand us over to the enemy just because the public outcry is so loud. Pilate did that when it came to Jesus: "Pilate sought to release him: but the Jews cried out, saying, If thou let this man go, thou art not Caesar's friend"

(v. 12). The people had spoken. Pilate, being a friend of the world, valued the cry of the murderer over the testimony of the Son of God. He honored the cry of the wicked. Scripture says "then delivered he him therefore unto them to be crucified" (v. 16).

The people rejected King Jesus and accepted as their king a mere man. The chief priests said, "We have no king but Caesar" (v. 15). Does that not sound like the uttering of an unbeliever in our current times? Today people are calling for us to be crucified. It would give them great pleasure to witness our demise. Are we greater than our Creator that the world should be rooting for us and not against us? No, we are not. Different people, different era, but hate is thriving—still! It is unsuccessful against the children of God. As children of God we must not cease doing good and spreading the gospel of truth. We will suffer losses, but God will reward us many times over.

Jesus was led to the slaughter by people who, no doubt, believed their hatred of Him was justified. They saw Him perform good deeds and miracles, but they hated Him nonetheless. If hate could cause the murder of a perfect man like Jesus, then it is understandable that people today carry around that same degree of hate for one another and use any excuse to become murderers of men. Hate justifies murder and then covers it up.

Hearts filled with contempt cannot feel. A murderous heart has no fellowship with God and therefore is empty of the Spirit of God. Hate doesn't lay down its life for a brother; love does that: "Hereby perceive we the love of God, because he laid down his life for us: and we ought to lay down our lives for the brethren" (1 John 3:16). When we believers come to know the price Jesus paid for us, it will be nearly impossible for us to take a life in cold blood and then justify it with a lying tongue. Instead we will realize that we gain eternal life by loving others, doing God's will, and laying down our own lives for others. Those are the ways of love.

We will be persecuted for following Christ and His teachings. Christians are hated in many places around the world. Rapidly rising is the number of believers in countries not well known for serving and worshipping God. The believers are being persecuted and killed. Their newfound love for "the way, truth, and the life" (John 14:6)—our Lord and Savior Jesus Christ—is being met with contempt. Christians are being hindered on their spiritual journey. Jesus warned us that serving Him would lead to hate: "And ye shall be hated of all men for my name's sake" (Matt. 10:22). The hate is going to be grievous to bear, "but he that endureth to the end shall be saved" (v. 22).

Our duty, if we want to live eternally with God, is to endure evil and not retaliate against it. Hate is born of hate. But we do not have to give in to hate. Hate does not have to become our reality. We all must realize we were made in the likeness of God and that we are all of one blood. Coming into that truth will allow us to shun the hate that counts other people as afterthoughts. Praying for those who embrace hatred allows us to walk in power and in authority. Hate can't defeat hate. Hating others because they hate us only makes matters worse.

Love and prayer can greatly diminish the power of evil in our lives. Loving the ones who hate us has a healing power. "Be not overcome of evil, but overcome evil with good" (Rom. 12:21), and, "Bless them which persecute you: bless, and curse not" (v. 14). Thus we have a charge to rise above hate, anger, division, and revenge. In Romans 12:17-20, Paul shows us the way to treat those who wrong us:

> Recompense to no man evil for evil. Provide things honest in the sight of all men. If it be possible, as much as lieth in you, live peaceably with all men. Dearly beloved, avenge not yourselves, but rather give place unto wrath: for it is written, Vengeance is mine; I will repay, saith the Lord. Therefore if thine enemy hunger, feed him; if he thirst, give him drink: for in so doing thou shalt heap coals of fire on his head.

Do you want to know how to defeat your enemy? Just remember those scriptures and live by their every word. And know that if people tell us it is okay to harm the ones who harm us or our loved ones, they are speaking against the instructions of the Lord, which means they are speaking the words of the devil. "Be kindly affectioned one to another with brotherly love; in honour preferring one another" (v. 10).

The book of wisdom discloses, "He that hideth hatred with lying lips, and he that uttereth a slander, is a fool" (Prov. 10:18). People know the hate that is in their hearts and will deny it to the end of time. Hate attacks and then hides its hand. That is why hate is so successful in creating division, oppressing the weak, and crushing the poor. Hate is comfortable in the dark. The hate-filled tongue will utter many evil things and then attempt to hide its venom by appealing to other hate-mongers. As poisonous and hateful as the utterances of fools might be, they have freedom of speech. So as much as we can, we must not give ear to their words. The important thing is making sure our own words are pleasing to God. "Let your speech be always with grace, seasoned with salt, that ye may know how ye ought to answer every man" (Col. 4:6).

God does want us to hate some things. We have been told we are never to hate our fellow man, but we are to hate sin and evil. In hating sin and evil, we cannot make the deadly mistake of hating the sinner. Throughout the Bible we are advised to hate evil: "The fear of the LORD is to hate evil: pride, and arrogancy, and the evil way, and the froward mouth, do I hate" (Prov. 8:13). It is also written, "Ye that love the LORD, hate evil" (Ps. 97:10). We, like the psalmist David, are to "hate and abhor lying" (Ps. 119:163). Hating sin and evil sets our souls on the right course to attaining eternal life. In regard to how we are supposed to feel about the world, we are not to love the world or any of the things in it, which would set us apart from the Divine One.

Just how much love does God have for us? "For God so loved the world, that he gave his only begotten Son, that whosoever believeth in him should not perish, but have everlasting life" (John 3:16). That is how much God loves us. Just how much are we to love God? "And thou shalt love the Lord thy God with all thy heart, and with all thy soul, and with all thy mind, and with all thy strength: this is the first commandment" (Mark 12:30). Last, how much are we to love our neighbor? "And the second is like, namely this, Thou shalt love thy neighbour as thyself. There is none other commandment greater than these" (v. 31). So that you will never forget how much God loves us, how much we are to love Him, and how we are supposed to love others, please write down and memorize those scriptures.

To love our fellow man, it is necessary that we view each other as human beings, created by one God who created all people of one blood. We all belong to the human race, although the world has divided us by assigning to us labels. Don't buy into the lie that we are somehow superior or inferior based on our race, ethnicity, or background. God "hath made of one blood all nations of men for to dwell on all the face of the earth, and hath determined the times before appointed, and the bounds of their habitation" (Acts 17:26). We are God's.

"And God said, Let us make man in our image, after our likeness" (Gen. 1:26). Genesis 1:27 then says that God went about creating "man in his own image, in the image of God created he him; male and female created he them." Get the picture? We are not freaks of nature, animals, or any derogatory thing. God said it. If a person says we are not all created of one blood, he is a child of the evil one and does not have eternal life in him. Do not argue this point, as Satan's children will not hear it. The Bible puts all the lies and myths to rest. We are created in the image of the One who made all things. Everything God made was good. God made no mistakes in His creations. We are to love God, love others, love ourselves, and let our actions and our speech glorify God!

Paul wrote, "Now I beseech you, brethren, mark them which cause divisions and offences contrary to the doctrine which ye have learned; and avoid them" (Rom. 16:17). When we know that someone is causing division that has nothing to do with God, we have to remove ourselves from that person. The evil one will never stop using willing participants to excite people to divide. "For they that are such serve not our Lord Jesus Christ, but their own belly; and by good words and fair speeches deceive the hearts of the simple" (v. 18). We cannot afford to be simple. We are under spiritual attack, and the devil is using everybody he can to get us to believe his lies.

Do not fret over the erupting volcanoes of hate that rain down destructive debris. Worry not yourselves because of all the evil going on in the world. Division, hate, and murders (in our homes, schools, workplaces, churches, communities, and among the nations and races) will continue and will grow worse as we near the end of this age. Our eyes and hearts should be fixed on God, our rock and shield. This is the devil's world. His house is standing on a sinking foundation and all who are a part of the house of evil will perish.

Satan's influence over the unbeliever is great. The unbeliever and the evildoer open their hearts to this influence. We cannot appeal to the spirit of darkness. It is a battle we must not engage in. "That which is crooked cannot be made straight" (Eccles. 1:15). Don't join in the battle of trying to prove what is wrong with the world to the world. They will never see it. In Proverbs 4:23, we are told, "Keep thy heart with all diligence; for out of it are the issues of life." Guarding our heart keeps it from hardening. Let us continue to grow in kindness, love, mercy, and compassion, remembering always that "Love worketh no ill to his neighbour" (Rom. 13:10). We can't lose by doing what God has instructed us to do. Love is the cure. Prayer is the answer. Jesus is the way.

7
A Generation of Vipers:
Part I

O generation of vipers, how can ye, being evil,
speak good things? for out of the abundance of
the heart the mouth speaketh.

Matt. 12:34

JESUS DIRECTED THIS open rebuke to the Pharisees, who had accused Him, saying, "This fellow doth not cast out devils, but by Beelzebub the prince of the devils" (Matt. 12:24). Their evil thoughts were not hidden from Jesus, and He addressed them accordingly. In falsely accusing Jesus of casting out devils by Beelzebub, the Pharisees had committed the unforgivable sin of blasphemy against the Holy Spirit.

Jesus cast out devils through the Holy Spirit. Jesus told His disciples that the Holy Spirit "shall teach you all things"

(John 14:26), "will guide you into all truth" (16:13), and "that he may abide with you for ever" (14:16). The Holy Spirit lives within those who believe in and accept Jesus, and He is our connection to Jesus and His teachings. Further, the Holy Spirit is "the Spirit of truth; whom the world cannot receive, because it seeth him not, neither knoweth him" (v.17). Denying and denouncing the Holy Spirit means eternal death. This eternal sin will not be forgiven.

One great thing about the Word of God is that it reveals the true nature of man. There is no smoke and mirrors. God does not hold back either. The Living Word exposes our unbelief and gives a perfect account of our wicked ways and our evil thoughts. We are much like the Pharisees of Jesus's day. God is speaking to us the same way He spoke to the Pharisees, because we are the new wicked generation proudly and arrogantly denying the power of God and the Holy Spirit that He sent to comfort us.

Our generation is looking for signs that God exists. To us, if we can't see it, then it must not exist. For God to be real, we want Him to come down in the flesh and meet us where we are, face-to-face. "If there is a God, why hasn't anyone seen Him?" the doubters say. We are no different than the Pharisees and the Sadducees who came together for Jesus to "shew them a sign from heaven" (Matt. 16:1). The Pharisees and the Sadducees were typically enemies, but they came together to oppose Jesus. That is the position of the world today. The unbeliever is saying, "I am self-made; I am my own god."

Jesus's answer to unbelievers looking for a sign is the same as when He walked among the people: "A wicked and adulterous generation seeketh after a sign; and there shall no sign be given unto it, but the sign of the prophet Jonas" (v. 4). Jonas's three days and three nights in the belly of the whale is a reference to how much time—three days and three nights—Jesus was to spend in the grave before His resurrection. Jesus explained, "For as Jonas was three days and three nights in the whale's belly; so shall the Son of man be three days and three nights in the heart of the earth" (12:40). Jesus is not going to send us a sign. We have His Word. Either we accept Him or we reject Him.

The reality is that God knows us better than we know ourselves. He knows when our hearts reject Him. To those of us who carry on like we are followers of God, the Lord says, "Forasmuch as this people draw near me with their mouth, and with their lips do honour me, but have removed their heart far from me" (Isa. 29:13). Who do we think we're fooling? It most certainly is not God. To Him our ways are well documented. We are vipers, sneaky and poisonous. There is something seriously wrong with us that God refers to us as vipers. Pay close attention to what God's Word says here: "And God saw that the wickedness of man was great in the earth, and that every imagination of the thoughts of his heart was only evil continually. And it repented the LORD that he had made man on the earth, and it grieved him at his heart" (Gen. 6:5-6). God grieves when we disobey Him. We have continued to disappoint him with our rejection of Him and our lack of love for one another.

We are living in trying times. This generation lives like it has no fear of God. We live in a time of explosive wickedness. If you look at someone the wrong way, that could mean the end of your life on earth. Sins and crimes are committed without regard to the eternal consequences. Satan has flipped off the light switch, and man has fallen into his trap. We are powerless because of our lack of faith. We are a "faithless and perverse generation" (Matt. 17:17). We are, in fact, a merciless generation ready to oppose, deny, and render judgment. The prophet Isaiah delivered a word of the Lord that also reads identical to who we are as a fallen nation and people. God addressed evildoers in the book of Isaiah as such: "Ah sinful nation, a people laden with iniquity, a seed of evildoers, children that are corrupters: they have forsaken the LORD, they have provoked the Holy One of Israel unto anger, they are gone away backward" (1:4).

We are born of evildoers. It is only in our own eyes, however, that we see ourselves as deserving and righteous beings. We tend to believe we are qualified, due to our delusions, to determine those people who deserve certain things and a certain type of treatment and who do not. In our own eyes we are above reproach. But if we think we are fooling God, we have another thought coming. How long will we continue to deceive ourselves and risk being totally separated from God because we have perverted God's Word and lived according to the world? Existing in the flesh and allowing the flesh to dictate our actions, we are nothing more than sinners who have given in to our own selfish desires. The stain of sin is on us. It is in us to do wrong, even when we are doing the right thing. Paul said it best:

> For I know that in me (that is, in my flesh,) dwelleth no good thing: for to will is present with me; but how to perform that which is good I find not. For the good that I would I do not: but the evil which I would not, that I do. Now if I do that I would not, it is no more I that do it, but sin that dwelleth in me. I find then a law, that, when I would do good, evil

is present with me. For I delight in the law of God after the inward man: But I see another law in my members, warring against the law of my mind, and bringing me into captivity to the law of sin which is in my members. (Rom. 7:18-23)

Further, "We are all as an unclean thing, and all our righteous-nesses are as filthy rags; and we all do fade as a leaf; and our iniq-uities, like the wind, have taken us away" (Isa. 64:6). By reason of truth, only God is qualified to judge, for He alone is perfect. We human beings are all just filthy rags with a false sense of how good we are. So that we do not make the mistake of assuming a self-righteous attitude, the Word of God must be burned into our hearts. We must accept the fact that on our own, we are unworthy to exalt ourselves above any other human being. We can use scripture as a measuring stick, as Jesus said: "there is none good but one, that is, God" (Mark 10:18).

In spite of all our wrongdoings, God loves us. It cannot be said enough that God hates sin, but He loves the sinner. I don't want anyone to confuse the two. God is always merciful and ready to forgive our sins. First, we have to know that we are committing sin, or at least be aware of what constitutes sin. We then have to be willing to confess our sins and to turn away from them. Therefore let us explore some things that make us poisonous to ourselves and to others, behaviors that open us up to destruction and make us the sons and daugh-ters of the evil one.

Unforgiveness
Lack of forgiveness is a poison that infects our entire being. A tremendous amount of energy is used in holding on to

a grudge. The weight of unforgiveness is heavy. The wrong done to us could be real or perceived. Either way, refusing to forgive destroys us little by little. Holding a grudge isn't always based on our experiencing the wrong firsthand. The "wrong" could be based on a rumor or an untruth. A person could hear a gossiper saying you spoke ill of him and then hold animosity toward you based on that gossiper's statement. It happens all the time. And you may never know why a person dislikes you, to the point that he or she avoids you at all cost. That is a sign of unforgiveness. And it goes against the Word of God. If we have a quarrel against someone, we are charged to be merciful toward each other and to forgive one another. Even as Christ forgave us, we are to do likewise (Col. 3:13).

"I just can't forgive him for that." Have you ever said this, or heard it uttered by a friend, acquaintance, family member, or stranger? It breaks my heart every time I hear someone say that they cannot forgive another person for what that person has done to them—or that something other than blasphemy against the Holy Spirit is unforgiveable. By closing our hearts and minds to forgiveness, we invite all forms of disasters into our own lives. Forgiving the individuals who wrong us, on the other hand, brings healing. A forgiving heart is a heart that pleases God.

Forgiveness isn't just saying with our mouths that we forgive someone. Anybody can claim to forgive. Forgiving means that we cleanse our hearts of all the ill will and resentment we have toward the person who wronged us. It means we have to stop talking about that individual in a negative manner and stop bringing up how the individual wronged us. When we forgive, we ought to be able to feel a lightness and a sense of peace in our hearts. Then, in the presence of the one who wronged us, we should be able to speak, to wish her well, and to feel no sense of awkwardness in her presence. True forgiveness allows us to move on in a hopeful way.

By choosing to hold on to the ugliness of unforgiveness, we disobey God. He cannot forgive us until we forgive those who have wronged us. Jesus commanded, "And when ye stand praying, forgive, if ye have ought against any: that your Father also which is in heaven may forgive you your trespasses" (Mark 11:25). Going through life holding a grudge against our neighbor carries a debilitating burden. Having an unforgiving heart jeopardizes our soul. We can't dwell with God if we die with unforgiveness still in our hearts. Jesus made that truth abundantly clear: "But if ye forgive not men their trespasses, neither will your Father forgive your trespasses" (Matt. 6:15).

Forgiveness is pardoning the trespasses of others against us and asking God, with a sincere heart, to pardon our sins against Him and against our neighbors. Let us not forget to forgive ourselves in the process! If you know anything about self-forgiveness, you know it takes work, just like forgiving others takes work. People will wrong us over and over again. Just think about how many times people have hurt you. You might wonder how many times you're required to forgive that person. The answer is "seventy times seven" (Matt. 18:22). That means there should be no limit to the number of times we forgive a person who trespasses against us. We are commanded to forgive as many times as it takes. If we are wronged a million times in our lifetime, we must forgive the perpetrator a million times. Forgiveness is a heart condition and must be done from the heart. God will do the rest.

Greed and the Love of Money

> But godliness with contentment is great gain. For we brought nothing into this world, and it is certain we can carry nothing out. And having food and raiment let us be therewith content. But they that will be rich fall into temptation and a snare, and into many foolish and hurtful lusts, which drown men in destruction and perdition. For the love of money is the root of all evil: which while some coveted after, they have erred from the faith, and pierced themselves through with many sorrows. But thou, O man of God, flee these things; and follow after righteousness, godliness, faith, love, patience, meekness. (1 Tim. 6:6-11)

Being in love with money is a sin that leads man down the road of temptation and traps him, bringing him misery and suffering. Although we are warned that the love of money is the root of all evil, that warning has hardly stopped man from loving money more than doing the will of God. I don't know how many times I've heard people talk about "chasing paper" or making the accumulation of wealth their primary goal. Millions of books about how to accumulate wealth are flying off bookstore shelves. One of the most popular topics in the world is how to get rich. "Get rich quick" is still the rave. The goal of achieving wealth seems to a bigger goal than having a relationship with God. Money, it is said, rules the world. The truth is that the *love* of money rules the people of the world. With man's insatiable desire for wealth, he bypasses God.

In this age of the Internet, it's not difficult to see how far down the path of destruction the love of money has taken us. People are willing to turn up the evil, as long as they are getting paid top dollar to do so. Human beings are selling their souls to the devil in exchange for riches and material possessions. Relationships and friendships mean nothing to the individual who sees wealth as the answer to everything. Goodwill toward mankind is thrown out the window when wealth is offered up as a replacement. The old and the young, worldwide, are falling into the trap, and are being swallowed up with sorrow.

The current atmosphere in today's society is geared toward getting rich. It has a lot to do with the images portrayed in magazines and on television. The rich have become the gods of this present day. They are seen as having power and having the world at their feet. It entices the rest of us to desire the same thing. We feel the rich do not have the troubles we have, because they can get whatever they want. The rich are showered with free stuff, while the poor can barely get a helping hand. And due to our continually falling away from God, generations are coming up that idolize riches and material possessions.

Also, the words of the rich are given weight. They are the invited speakers at graduation ceremonies and the subjects of interviews on television shows. The masses want to hear their opinions, which are valued over real wisdom. Millions of people cry out in admiration at the sight of the rich and famous. The rich have more admirers and followers than God, it seems!

The poor and needy are overlooked and despised. Have you ever seen a poor man deliver a commencement address at a graduation? I haven't. Are poor people, those struggling to make ends meet, considered successful by anyone you know? Are they considered "esteemed" at the church you attend? Are they given front-row seats anywhere you go? No. These things are not commonplace in regard to the poor. Poor men are not accepted and definitely not shown the same courtesy as rich men. You don't see poor people being profiled as models of success in the magazines or being asked for advice or being valued for the simple fact that they are human. Instead the poor are despised. In James 2:5-7, we can get a picture of the rich versus the poor:

> Hearken, my beloved brethren, Hath not God chosen the poor of this world rich in faith, and heirs of the kingdom which he hath promised to them that love him? But ye have despised the poor. Do not rich men oppress you, and draw you before the judgment seats? Do not they blaspheme that worthy name by the which ye are called?

The rich appear to have it all. And for the most part (here on earth, at least), they do. Things, things, and more things! People fall on their knees to give them more things, free things. Hands are open to them but closed to the poor. The wealthy go about their everyday lives with very little concern about what they're going to eat, where they're going to lay their heads, what they're going to drive, what they're going to wear, or how they're going to pay their bills. They have a certain level of trust in their wealth. Hear me carefully! I am not saying it is a sin to possess wealth. God blesses us so that we have the means to live comfortably and to bless others who are in need. God is not against us having money and enjoying it. He is against greed and selfishness. He is against the rich turning a blind eye to the poor and needy. God is against oppressing the needy and putting money above all else.

Many rich people have said that God is a figment of poor people's imagination. This is part of the reason some of them despise the poor. The devil, being the con artist he is, cons them into believing that because they are rich, they are their own gods. What the lovers of money don't seem to understand is that the devil has duped them into believing they should put their confidence in their wealth and that they can rely on themselves and themselves alone to make their own way in this world. God is not given the credit. Man takes the credit for himself. This, though, is what the Bible teaches us to do regarding the rich: "Charge them that are rich in this world, that they be not highminded, nor trust in uncertain riches, but in the living God, who giveth us richly all things to enjoy; That they do good, that they be rich in good works, ready to distribute, willing to communicate" (1 Tim. 6:17-18).

Notice that God is the One who liberally gives us all things for our enjoyment, including money! However, He commands the rich to be ready to give, with an open heart and outstretched hand. He wants them to be generous in doing good deeds and to be willing to share their resources when asked or when they see someone in need.

Being financially poor all my life, I have spent a lot of time around other poor people. Most of them have one other thing in common: *they want to be rich*. I've heard so many of them say, "I would do anything to be rich." I had that same mindset once upon a time. I remember when the lottery first made its appearance in the state of Georgia. People flocked to the stores, standing in long lines, waiting for their chance to win a piece of the pot. The lines consisted mostly of the unemployed, the underemployed, and the working class. I was working in a convenience store at the time, and I too was hooked on the lottery. I just remember feeling desperate financially. And I wanted to put an end to my struggling. The lottery seemed to offer us a chance to get out of our current financial rut. Hope was the trick! It gave us a *false hope*. While God wanted us to put our trust in Him, we put our trust in luck. We fell into the trap set by the devil. Poor people became poorer. And the desperation to rise from poverty to riches continues even today.

Yes, the lottery was making a tiny number of people wealthy, but poor people are still looking for their break, still talking about what they would do if they were to win the lottery. But gambling is just one tool the devil uses to entice people with riches. Stealing from others, running scams, engaging in fraud, making a mockery of oneself, and using other such tactics for personal gain are all tools of the devil.

With our eyes set and our minds focused on winning the jackpot by any means, we fall into all sorts of traps because we are walking in darkness, chasing after riches, and running away from God. Satan is happy to see us doing this because he knows that when we are desperate for material possessions and anything outside of the kingdom of God, he doesn't have to do much to claim our souls. He knows that hundreds of millions of people are ignoring God's Word: "Labour not to be rich" (Prov. 23:4). There is no spiritual satisfaction in chasing wealth. Greed is an empty hole. You could throw as much stuff and money as you want into it, and it will still be an empty hole. The rich cannot be rich enough, and the poor cannot do enough to get rich.

I have seen many people fall because of their desire to be rich. They seek out and try every get-rich-quick scheme they can. Some get into selling drugs because it's quick money and the world of drugs is glamorized. Because this is a trick of the devil, people don't see that it's a trap. Then there are the credit card scams, welfare fraud, bootlegging, selling stolen merchandise, and identity theft. The poor and desperate have come up with endlessly inventive ways to steal a piece of the financial pie. There are scams too numerous to mention. More scams are being invented and other scams are being improved upon. Scams abound because people are desperate to bite into the prosperity pie. The love of money provides the motivation.

The devil will continue his assault on the greedy and on those who love money more than they love doing good deeds. The greedy will always be enticed by the devil's get-rich-quick schemes. According to the scripture (Col. 3:5), greed is idolatry. Fully knowing man's level of greed, God in His Word addressed on many occasions the dangers that come with great possessions and riches. God knows that the level of our selfishness is high.

Attachment to wealth is not confined to the unbeliever. Believers also fall in love with riches. They could have everything else lined up with the teachings of Jesus and be lacking in that they rely on their riches and perhaps don't do enough to help the poor. Think about the rich young ruler in Mark 10:17 who approached Jesus and asked, "Good Master, what shall I do that I may inherit eternal life?" This young man knew and kept the commandments, but he was lacking one thing in living a full spiritual life. Jesus answered him, saying, "One thing thou lackest: go thy way, sell whatsoever thou hast, and give to the poor, and thou shalt have treasure in heaven: and come, take up the cross, and follow me" (v. 21). What do you think would happen if Jesus told a rich person today to sell all he owns and give it to the poor? The modern rich man would probably think Jesus had lost His mind. The selfish spirit does not let go of anything. We all know people who wouldn't give a poor person a quarter, much less everything he has in his possession.

And concerning the rich young ruler? He "was sad at that saying, and went away grieved: for he had great possessions" (v. 22). Even Jesus's disciples didn't know what to make of the Lord's words. The Bible says "the disciples were astonished" (v. 24) at His statement that it was hard for the rich to enter God's kingdom, so Jesus repeated Himself in the same verse: "Children, how hard is it for them that trust in riches to enter into the kingdom of God!" They remained silent, perhaps looking around at each other and waiting for someone else to reply. Not one of the disciples said anything, though. Instead Jesus followed up with, "It is easier for a camel to go through the eye of a needle, than for a rich man to enter into the kingdom of God" (v. 25). That sounds like a really small chance to me. Twisting the scripture to justify one's love of money and possessions will not make this or any other scripture less true.

How will the rich explain to God how they stored up their millions and billions, lived in the lap of luxury, and ate from the fatted calf while their fellow men and women were destitute, homeless, and hungry? What excuse will they come up with to justify not doing all they can to make life a little more bearable for the poor? If we truly desire to live a godly life, it would be beneficial to ask ourselves if we are doing everything we can do to be a blessing to others. God knows what means we have and how capable we are of being a blessing to others.

God commands that we use our resources to do good. He doesn't put conditions on our giving. Too often I hear or read comments by people who say they refuse to give to the "lazy," as they clump just about everyone in need in that category. Only man sets limits and stipulations on giving. We are expected by God to give, whether the poor person has a job or not. If our enemy is in need, we are directed by God to give to him. The Bible teaches, "If thine enemy be hungry, give him bread to eat; and if he be thirsty, give him water to drink" (Prov. 25:21). If we are told by God to give to our enemies, shouldn't we also be quick to give to strangers in need?

Giving of our time and resources is something we all should do. No one is excluded from giving to the poor and supporting the weak. Mankind has a responsibility to serve one another. The church is not excluded either. The church is in fact charged with providing for those who are unable to provide for themselves. The apostle Paul shared the following message with the church elders regarding giving: "I have shewed you all things, how that so labouring ye ought to support the weak, and to remember the words of the Lord Jesus, how he said, It is more blessed to give than to receive" (Acts 20:35). The church has a responsibility to make provision for the weak.

Too much wealth exists in the world for anyone to be without food, clothing, health care, or shelter. However, go anywhere on earth, and you will find the poor. It's ungodly that any man or woman or child is homeless or hungry. Investments are not being made in people unless they have some special talent that the investor knows will bring him a substantial return. Other than that we are slow to invest in our brothers and sisters. "For the poor shall never cease out of the land: therefore I command thee, saying, Thou shalt open thine hand wide unto thy brother, to thy poor, and to thy needy, in thy land" (Deut. 15:11). Although Moses delivered this message from God to the Israelites, the message is meant for us also. We should always have an open hand, not a hardened heart, toward the poor and needy. This is God's command. Helping our brothers and sisters in need pleases God. In return God blesses us.

Giving is the enemy to the greedy and selfish. Greed prevents us from tithing. In our giving we have an obligation to give to the house of God through tithing. I don't think we have quite gotten the message on tithing yet. It is probably one of the biggest reasons people do not attend church. Oh, the grumbling, complaining, and mocking that takes place when the word "tithing" is spoken! The topic of tithing has led to many a debate. Somehow the majority of us have come to see tithing as making it possible for a preacher to live in luxury as the congregation remains in poverty. This is how we know Satan has, again, worked his con game on us. We fail to see the whole picture. Tithing is something God has commanded us to do. We learn this in Malachi 3:10: "Bring ye all the tithes into the storehouse, that there may be meat in mine house."

Tithing pleases the Lord. Refusing to tithe is robbing God: "Will a man rob God? Yet ye have robbed me. But ye say, Wherein have we robbed thee? In tithes and offerings" (v. 8). Hardships are likely to abound when we do not tithe. The scripture says, "Ye are cursed with a curse: for ye have robbed me, even this whole nation" (v. 9). Reliance on money keeps us from giving and tithing. Refusing to tithe is being disobedient to God. That disobedience brings upon us many troubles.

Numerous scriptures teach us the dangers of possessing riches, neglecting to care for the poor and needy, and failing to share our resources with others. Selfishness is not of God. It is a trait of the children of the devil. And when we venture into the territory of storing up our treasures here on earth, we close our hearts to the will of God. Here are some scriptures to study and to hold deep within your heart so that you are guarded against trusting in wealth and material possessions:

- "But woe unto you that are rich! for ye have received your consolation" (Luke 6:24). The comfort of the rich is their riches and the luxuries their wealth affords them. Their consolation is temporary, because it comes from the world. If they put their faith in their riches, they will receive no consolation from the Lord.
- "Lay not up for yourselves treasures upon earth, where moth and rust doth corrupt, and where thieves break through and steal: But lay up for yourselves treasures in heaven, where neither moth nor rust doth corrupt, and where thieves do not break through nor steal: For where your treasure is, there will your heart be also" (Matt. 6:19-21). Earthly treasures are as temporary as life itself. Things deteriorate, diminish in value, and are stolen. Jesus wants our focus to be heavenward and not on the things of the earth, because He knows that whatever we trust in, that is what we worship. Worshippers of things are separated from God.

- "He that trusteth in his riches shall fall; but the righteous shall flourish as a branch" (Prov. 11:28). Notice the word *righteous*! That means we have to live according to the Word of God. Blameless! We cannot go to God any kind of way and expect Him to cause us to flourish. If we want to experience the fullness of God, it is mandatory that we turn from sin.

- "Whoso stoppeth his ears at the cry of the poor, he also shall cry himself, but shall not be heard" (Prov. 21:13). God requires that we give ear to the poor, that we do not disregard them, and that we hear their cry for help. Whatever we do for the poor, God will do for us. If we turn a deaf ear to the poor, God will not hear us when we cry out to Him. Helping the poor is doing the will of God.

- "... if riches increase, set not your heart upon them" (Ps. 62:10). We are not to fall in love with wealth. Loving riches corrupts the heart.

- "But God said unto him, Thou fool, this night thy soul shall be required of thee: then whose shall those things be, which thou hast provided? So is he that layeth up treasure for himself, and is not rich toward God" (Luke 12:20-21). A rich man is said to be a fool if he views his wealth as his security blanket. That is scripture. He stores up riches for himself and closes his hands to the poor. The rich man gives God no credit. He doesn't realize that one day he will die and have to answer to God for his selfish ways.

- "Let your conversation be without covetousness; and be content with such things as ye have: for he hath said, I will never leave thee, nor forsake thee" (Heb.

13:5). Again, chasing riches displeases God. We are encouraged to be happy with what we already have. God wants us to trust in Him and Him alone, and have faith that He will be with us always. He will provide His children with all they need.

• "... let not the rich man glory in his riches: But let him that glorieth glory in this, that he understandeth and knoweth me, that I am the Lᴏʀᴅ which exercise loving-kindness, judgment, and righteousness, in the earth: for in these things I delight, saith the Lᴏʀᴅ" (Jer. 9:23-24). The Lord tells us not to take pride in nor trust in riches. Remember, loving the world and the things in the world puts us at odds with God! Taking pride in wealth and material possessions is akin to idol worship. In worshipping money we walk in darkness. If we are to glory in anything, it's knowing God intimately and trusting in His way.

God is not a selfish God. He doesn't want us, His children, to be selfish either. God wants us to be givers, not takers. It pleases God when we guard our hearts from becoming hardened against our neighbors in need. We need to be approachable, kindhearted, and giving. Just as God owns everything and gives to man freely, so should man give freely. The greedy and selfish have their reward on earth. Those of us who believe and trust in God know that earthly possessions are temporary. Glorifying fame, fortune, and material possessions only leads to destruction.

Idol Worship
God has made His stance on idol worship abundantly clear. He forbids engaging in idol worship. He is a jealous God, and He

does not take kindly to man, whom He created, worshipping false gods. Let us take a closer look at what God commanded in regard to idol worship:

> Thou shalt have no other gods before me. Thou shalt not make unto thee any graven image, or any likeness of any thing that is in heaven above, or that is in earth beneath, or that is in the water under the earth. Thou shalt not bow down thyself to them, nor serve them: for I the LORD thy God am a jealous God, visiting the iniquity of the fathers upon the children unto the third and fourth generation of them that hate me.... (Exod. 20:3-5)

Idol worship gives glory to some image or other thing with no power against the all-powerful God. Idol gods could be statues or any graven image or a human or any number of things worshipped by man. Idol gods replace the true God in the lives of the ungodly. God is not hard-pressed that we should worship Him. Although He has sent out a grave warning to idol worshippers everywhere, He has also given them the right to serve whomever they please. God gives us commandments to follow but also the space to follow and to serve whom we want. And, boy, have we taken the path that leads away from God, worshipping everything from rain and a little potbelly statue to power, fame, money, and entertainment.

To some people God is a joke. I mentioned earlier that a young man told me, "I see God in the same way I see Santa Claus. He's just a figment of the imagination. I don't believe in God." Unfortunately millions of people the world over see God as a figment of others' imaginations. Paul said that man "changed the glory of the uncorruptible God into an image made like to corruptible man, and to birds, and fourfooted beasts, and creeping things" (Rom. 1:23). This is what man has reduced God to. They have made their own selfish desires their gods. The psalmist laments that unbelievers' "idols are silver and gold, the work of men's hands" (Ps. 115:4).

Witchcraft and Fortune-telling

Witchcraft and fortune-telling are practices in evil. Their place is in darkness. God strictly forbids the practice of witchcraft (which includes sorcery, spells, superstition, horoscopes, supernatural magic, the invocation of spirits, etc.) and fortune-telling (telling someone's future through the use of a psychic, clairvoyant, or soothsayer, to include palm-reading, gazing into a crystal ball, etc.). These acts attempt to explore the unknown by consulting powers of darkness. Any form of witchcraft or fortune-telling is the work of the devil and his agents. The practitioners and those who consult them do not have eternal life dwelling within them, because these things are abominations to the Lord:

> There shall not be found among you any one that maketh his son or his daughter to pass through the fire, or that useth divination, or an observer of times, or an enchanter, or a witch, or a charmer, or a consulter with familiar spirits, or a wizard, or a necromancer. For all that do these things are an abomination unto the Lord.... (Deut. 18:10-12)

The world is crying out for a sign. God is not going to give us another sign. We have to have faith that Jesus died for our sins, was raised on the third day with all power in His hand,

and has gone to prepare a place for those of us who love and believe in Him. God also sent the Holy Spirit to guide us on our walk through this life. He is all we need. However, if we don't believe God has given us all we need, our crying out will be met with silence. Unbelievers (to include "Christians" who consult with darkness because they don't believe in the power of the Almighty) will look for answers everywhere except in the One who gave them life. It is no wonder they are turning to the devil for answers, and the devil is leading them deeper into the abyss. True believers know and put their trust in God.

You will find practitioners of witchcraft and fortune-telling in nearly every corner of the world. They advertise their services like any other profitable business ("profitable" in terms of money only). Many of them have targeted Christians by using Bible verses or by including God in their conversations. It is a slick tactic the devil uses to trap the unwise Christian believer. The devil is smart and is constantly updating his game plan.

Witchcraft has tricked many souls into buying in, and the practice has been extremely successful in winning over "Christians." I have known people (and still do), so-called Christians and active church attendees, who believe heavily in witchcraft and are always performing some ritual to fight against people they believed were trying to put roots (aka spells) on them. They say, "I believe (insert name here) is trying to put roots on me." So they find a root doctor to give them a remedy against the root or spell. Because of their belief in witchcraft and its power, some of those people have lost touch with reality. People in the church are falling hard for this trick of the devil. One minute they are Christians; the next minute they are entertaining the works of the devil and his agents.

An extremely popular form of witchcraft is the invocation of spirits or communicating with the dead. Numerous television shows and commercials have showcased the work of mediums, clairvoyants, necromancers, and people who practice divination. The blind swarm to these shows and seek the services of these people who dare to dance with the devil. It would be laughable how gullible human beings are when it comes to their romancing witchcraft—if it were not so real. They are easily tricked, because the devil knows their desire for the unknown is not able to be satisfied. So he sends his angels to infect greedy people who know they can get great financial gain, and to contaminate the desperate souls searching for the unknown. The living know one thing concerning the future: "that they shall die" (Eccles. 9:5). Moreover:

> ... but the dead know not any thing, neither have they any more a reward; for the memory of them is forgotten. Also their love, and their hatred, and their envy, is now perished; neither have they any more a portion for ever in any thing that is done under the sun. (vv. 5-6)

We are further told "... there is no work, nor device, nor knowledge, nor wisdom, in the grave, whither thou goest" (v. 10). The dead know nothing. They cannot communicate with any living human being. They are not looking down on us with a watchful eye, but God is, and only He is able to do that. Do not ever be confused that anyone can contact another who has passed on from this life. It is impossible. Do not be deceived by the workers of darkness!

Fortune-telling and divining one's future based on astrology and horoscopes all fall into a similar category as witchcraft. They may seem innocent and fun, but their origin is evil. Again, searching for the unknown is declaring the devil our god. The people offering these services can tell us one thing about our future: we are going to die. That is the extent of their knowledge regarding future happenings.

Then there are superstitions! Superstitions are useless. They run the gamut so wide and far that they could fill a book. Superstitions are practiced by many in the church too. One cannot be a true believer in God and live a superstitious lifestyle. Believers would do well to remember that superstitions are the works of the wicked, and there is no power to them. Practicing superstitious behaviors does not cause one to win at sports, but being the better team does. There is no luck in entertaining superstitious behaviors. The devil would have you believe the lie that engaging superstitious behaviors gives us an advantage in life. It does not. What it does is set us at odds with God.

Every human being was created by God, but every human being is not a child of God; many are children of the devil. The children of the devil do his work, attempting always to turn people away from the truth, like when Elymas opposed Barnabas and Saul, who had been "sent forth by the Holy Ghost" (Acts 13:4). The devil and his children never cease from trying to prevent us from hearing the Word of God. When someone is seeking to know God, the devil has a lie ready to throw into the mix. He does not disappoint in this regard:

... the deputy of the country, Sergius Paulus, a prudent man; who called for Barnabas and Saul, and desired to hear the word of God. But Elymas the sorcerer (for so is his name by interpretation) withstood them, seeking to turn away the deputy from the faith. Then Saul, (who also is called Paul,) filled with the Holy Ghost, set his eyes on him. And said, O full of all subtilty and all mischief, thou child of the devil, thou enemy of all righteousness, wilt thou not cease to pervert the right ways of the Lord? (vv. 7-10)

Looking for answers from anyone other than God is not a wise thing to do. The answers you are going to get are lies from the devil. Seeking the advice of a worker of witchcraft is like dining at the table of the wicked one: your portion will be poison.

Scripture warns, "Ye cannot drink the cup of the Lord, and the cup of devils: ye cannot be partakers of the Lord's table, and of the table of devils" (1 Cor. 10:21). We are also advised to "have no fellowship with the unfruitful works of darkness, but rather reprove them" (Eph. 5:11). God's Word also cries out to us: "Beloved, follow not that which is evil, but that which is good. He that doeth good is of God: but he that doeth evil hath not seen God" (3 John 1:11). God has spoken. His Word is the first and the last. If we desire to be with Him, our beliefs and deeds have to line up with scripture.

8
A Generation of Vipers: Part II

SCRIPTURE GETS IT right (of course) when it speaks to us about each age of humanity: "There is a generation that are pure in their own eyes, and yet is not washed from their filthiness" (Prov. 30:12). We are living in an era when men and women are righteous in their own eyes. Because they deceive themselves into believing that they have high moral standards, they think they are qualified to say who is righteous and who is not. Usually they place themselves above the average human being. I can tell you now, they will be surprised when they face God, only for God to turn them away and sentence them to eternal torment. A hypocrite might fool the world, because the world is blind. He will deceive himself into believing that he is godly. However, God, who tries the heart, will not be tricked into believing the lies of man.

We, being filthy rags ourselves, think we have the know-it-all to appoint others worthy, or deserving, or God's anointed. But we are judging the outward appearance. It's been happening since the beginning of time. Even when God was in the process of choosing a king to rule over Israel, the prophet/ priest Samuel thought he knew exactly whom God would choose. Samuel "looked on Eliab, and said, Surely the LORD's anointed is before him" (1 Sam. 16:6). Samuel did the same thing we do today in choosing a "worthy" candidate. However, God shut him down: "But the LORD said unto Samuel, Look not on his countenance, or on the height of his stature; because I have refused him: for the LORD seeth not as man seeth; for man looketh on the outward appearance, but the LORD looketh on the heart" (v. 7).

God rejected seven of Jesse's sons. God chose David. This was an unexpected choice, because David wasn't ever considered by Samuel or Jesse. Man overlooked David and might have even been ashamed of David or to be seen with him. God, however, saw that David was fearless and worthy and that David was the best person for the job. Right now the world might be refusing you, saying you are not worthy or qualified, but God is looking at you, favoring you, and choosing you, because He knows that you are fearless and worthy and the absolute best candidate for the position. We can never allow man to determine our worth or simply agree to man's assessment of us. God either chooses us or rejects us, based on His assessment of our hearts. And that is the real and true test.

We go about our days living according to our own ways, which we see as being right, but yet we are filthy, sinful, and hypocritical, because how we look to the world takes precedence over how we look to God—desiring the praise, attention, and accolades the world has to offer. So we carry on, speaking one thing and doing another. In our hearts the world is what we love, and God does not reside in our thoughts. We are a generation of vipers, poisonous and unforgiving. Our hearts and minds are filled with filth, but we will not take the time to make sure we are right before God. We would rather put down our fellow man and keep up a "good" and "acceptable" front to impress our neighbors than to fall on our knees, repent, and turn from the wickedness that binds us to eternal damnation.

In the previous chapter we took a look at the poisons that separate us from the will of God. We discussed such poisons as witchcraft, idol worship, greed, selfishness, and unforgiveness. Indulgence in sin separates us from God and positions us under the controlling thumb of the devil. In such a position, we remain enemies with God and are on a direct path to the bottomless pit, the future home for those of us who do not live for the Lord. Let's look at a few more poisons that trap us.

Hypocrisy

Without the proper tools, it is difficult to read man, as he is a complex creature. He can put on many faces and can have us believe the face he presents in public. That public face is the one we use to measure a person. How a person interacts with us is basically the only thing we have to go on—well, that, and hearsay. But if we have understanding, we know that rumors cannot and should not be counted for anything.

Separating man's actions from his words should not be a difficult task. We have to be observant at all times, measuring a person's actions and words using the Word of God. The question we must always ask ourselves is this: "Does his or her actions and words line up with scripture?" The conniving person who appears to be upstanding, and whose talk seems to align with the favorable façade he presents to the public, could trick anyone, whether a believer or an unbeliever. For example, a married politician who has worked hard to present the image of a loyal and loving family man with the successful and devoted wife and happy and well-adjusted children can work tirelessly to promote the sanctity of marriage and the importance of family as part of his campaign, yet successfully hide an adulterous relationship and a broken home from the public. A person can craft whatever image he chooses and live a secret life that is totally opposite of the image he has crafted for public acceptance. You could probably name several occasions when a person has fought against something only to be found out as a part of that thing he's fought against. Therefore we will need every bit of understanding we can get in order to deal successfully with the hypocrite.

Hypocrites abound. They love to hear themselves talk. Their enjoyment and satisfaction come from being able to hide, if only briefly, in the dark. Their words make them appear godly. They elevate themselves above their neighbors, shining the light on the sins of others and covering up their own with much speech. To hear her tell it, the hypocrite is against every evil behavior, but she is likely engaging in the very same. The hypocrite is able to fool those who hold him in high regard. He is able to trick himself into believing his own lies too. His reward comes in the form of votes, pats on the back, and approval from those who are impressed by him. But to those who walk in the light of truth, he is like an open book.

The hypocrite constructs a high throne for himself and commences to pass judgment on others. She exalts herself above her sisters; he, above his brothers. Hypocrites are no different from the Pharisee who went up into the temple along with a publican to pray, as Jesus related in a parable: "The Pharisee stood and prayed thus with himself, God, I thank thee, that I am not as other men are, extortioners, unjust, adulterers, or even as this publican" (Luke 18:11). Like the Pharisee, the hypocrite is just in his own eyes. But God knows his heart and is neither impressed nor convinced.

The Pharisee in the parable, because he did not believe himself to be a sinner, did not ask God to forgive him. He stood in his own way. The publican, on the other hand, knew he was a sinner. His prayer was, "God be merciful to me a sinner" (v. 13). The parable ends with Jesus saying, "I tell you, this man went down to his house justified rather than the other: for every one that exalteth himself shall be abased; and he that humbleth himself shall be exalted" (v. 14). Hypocrites hurt themselves. There is earthly gain in their actions, yes. But heaven will not be their reward. We would do good to pray, like the publican, to God that He forgives us our sins and shows us mercy.

I remember working with a young man who, in human estimation, was a pretty good fellow. One day he and another staff member were talking about a famous boxer. The young man began to say how much he despised the boxer. He said, "I don't like him because he is a horrible person. He is the lowest form of a person I know. He beats on every woman he dates. He doesn't deserve to breathe the same air as we do." I wasn't so much shocked by his words as I was saddened by his exalting himself above another human being.

The young man's words caught my attention because I had never heard him talk like that. I didn't expect to hear my coworker put down another person, because I knew something about the young man that a lot of other people probably didn't know. The young man had once opened up to me and to a couple other trusted employees about his drug use. He admitted to us that he'd done some pretty bad things. We all shared a lot that evening, and on other occasions he also shared with me. He was not only a current drug user, but also an alcoholic. He made constant visits to his doctor to get his drug of choice. His struggle with substance abuse was obvious.

So upon hearing my coworker bash the boxer, I volunteered my two cents' worth and said, "We are no better than he is, because we have all done wrong."

"I am better than he is. You can't get any worse than a man who hits on women," the young man replied.

"How can you say what another person deserves, and who are we to say we are better than another human being anyway?" I asked.

The young man repeated that he was better than the famous boxer and that he was nothing like him. I didn't argue with him further, but I was seething inside because I understood that it is not our place to elevate ourselves over another person, and so I could not judge him as he had judged the boxer. However, he did not have the same level of understanding, and therefore would not accept what I was saying. Unfortunately millions of people have the same kind of thinking: "I am better than her because she does this and I do that." In other words people tell themselves that their sins are not as bad as other people's sins. Such people serve the god of hypocrisy. Trying to break down that wall of hypocrisy would do us more harm than good. The hypocrite would simply argue against wisdom.

Pointing out someone else's faults hinders our own journey to being better people. Yet the hypocrite is always telling someone what they should or shouldn't do, how to conduct oneself, and how they are so different from everybody else. But Jesus said:

> And why beholdest thou the mote that is in thy brother's eye, but considerest not the beam that is in thine own eye? Or how wilt thou say to thy brother, Let me pull out the mote out of thine eye; and, behold, a beam is in thine own eye? Thou hypocrite, first cast out the beam out of thine own eye; and then shalt thou see clearly to cast out the mote out of thy brother's eye. (Matt. 7:3-5)

We must first focus on getting ourselves right with God before we go trying to instruct others on what is right and telling them how they should live. We cannot see clearly because our own lives are bogged down in sin, but we are quick to jump on our high horses and ride over to someone else's house to sweep around her door. It does not work that way. Let us clean the skeletons out of our own closets first. If we can do that, then we will put ourselves in a situation to get some of that unlimited favor God is so gracious to give us. But we cannot get it by keeping our heads buried in somebody else's affairs.

Hypocrisy shows up in many ways. Man loves to be praised. He loves it when he is elevated by other human beings. When we do something for people, we want the world to know. Hypocrisy screams, "Look what I did! Did anybody see me?" Oh, how social media document the hypocrisy in our "good" deeds! You see pictures of people taking the shoes off their feet and the clothes off their backs, giving them to the homeless. I've seen videos of people feeding and giving things to the needy. You name the "good" deed, it turns up on social media and in news outlets everywhere. Such a showing makes some people instant celebrities. Their reward is their fifteen minutes of fame.

I was recently browsing a social media platform when I came across a video that showed a man handing out money, food, and drinks to people lying on the sidewalk in front of the store he was visiting. This man was followed closely by a cameraman who recorded the giver as he did his "good" deeds. As the cameraman continued recording, the giver turned and spoke to the camera. Later the giver uploaded the video to his social media page. I read many comments that piled kind words upon the giver. Some people referred to the man as a wonderful person. A few said that it is why they respect him so much. Others said he has a good heart. A number of viewers said they cried after watching his acts of kindness. Some told him that God was going to bless him for what he did. They were wrong. The giver had already received all the blessings he'd get. His "blessings," if you could call them that, were the praises he received from people.

While watching this video, I had a scripture immediately come to mind. Being able to call on a scripture to test another person's spirit is so important. We can always count on scripture to reveal what otherwise wouldn't be revealed. The teaching was this:

> Therefore when thou doest thine alms, do not sound a trumpet before thee, as the hypocrites do in the synagogues and in the streets, that they may have glory of men. Verily I say unto you, They have their reward. (Matt. 6:2)

When giving gets to be a show, God is not getting the glory. Man is getting the glory. The compliments of men warmed this man's heart and made him feel like he was doing something special. God does not even take note of such deeds. These deeds are done in vain.

When it comes to hypocrisy, there is just as much of it in the church as out in the world. There are people in the church filled with hypocrisy. They talk about their love for God and how God is the head of their lives. Their prayers are long and drawn-out to impress men. But Jesus cautioned us about long, loud prayers: "And when thou prayest, thou shalt not be as the hypocrites are: for they love to pray standing in the synagogues and in the corners of the streets, that they may be seen of men. Verily I say unto you, They have their reward" (Matt. 6:5).

The hypocrite makes the world his stage. He lives for the praise of people. If he's a preacher, he stands in the pulpit of the church and puts on a show for the people. The praise that people heap on him will be his reward. He will not receive anything from the Lord. The same words Jesus spoke to the scribes and the Pharisees in Matthew 15:7-9, he speaks to the hypocrites of today: "Ye hypocrites, well did Esaias prophesy of you, saying, This people draweth nigh unto me with their mouth, and honoureth me with their lips; but their heart is far from me. But in vain they do worship me, teaching for doctrines the commandments of men."

That is hypocrisy at its best. Today's hypocrites continue the tradition of worshipping God with their mouths while their hearts are not with God. Their lives are out of sync with the teachings of the gospel. They also teach things that appease man and things that man would rather hear instead of the gospel of truth. The hypocrite receives a bad report from Jesus.

Nearly the entire twenty-third chapter of Matthew calls out hypocrites, with Jesus saying they are "fools and blind" (Matt. 23:17, 19) and admonishing them for the evil they do. Surely hypocrisy goes against the wise teachings of the gospel of truth. God frowns upon hypocrisy. God's assessment of the hypocrite is this: "Even so ye also outwardly appear righteous unto men, but within ye are full of hypocrisy and iniquity" (v. 28). Don't be alarmed when someone judges you. Just remember what the gospel has to say about the hypocrite: they may have the appearance of a righteous man, but they are sinful hypocrites. That tells me they don't have what it takes to judge us.

Gossip and a Lying Tongue
How gossip sells! The best-selling reading material is full of gossip, rumors, and lies. Television has no shortage of gossip shows. Gossip is the biggest form of entertainment among the lost. Never mind that it hurts people! Never mind that it may be full of treacherous lies! As long as gossip entertains the masses, that is what's important. Gossip and lies go hand in hand. Once gossip or a lie gets started, it can go on for years. It seems more socially acceptable to believe the gossip or the lie than to seek the truth. This is because gossip seems more exciting than truth. It's juicy, mouth-watering food to the evildoer. The gossiper is applauded for her ability to dish out gossip in a way that has listeners hanging off the edge of their seats.

You can take your pick of the so-called entertainers and TV stars whose shows are filled with nothing but gossip. An abundance of gossip is available to audiences whose ears are burning for anything related to disaster. They soak up lies and gossip like a sponge soaks up water. And it seems to make them happy to hear about the downfall of others. Gossip gives life to the walking dead. They can hardly wait to hear the latest gossip on their favorite celebrities and reality stars, on public officials and politicians, on CEOs and anyone else such gossip and lies would hurt the most.

For at least an hour every day the walking dead can forget about their problems. They live and breathe gossip, even if the gossip is a blatant lie. They do not care, as long as some-one's life is being turned upside down by it. They go so far as to defend the gossiper, saying, "I like her, because she tells it like it is and she doesn't care who it is." Such a statement speaks to just how lost people are, thinking that gossip is a good thing. When an individual can go around and make gos-siping a lifestyle, not caring who they hurt in the process, he or she is a murderer. Also, the person whose feet run to hear it, he is just as guilty.

The gossiper has no desire to control the destruction that falls from his lips. His ways are a disappointment to God. Gossiping folks choose to contribute to the devastation of a life and will never participate in the uplifting of their neighbor in truth. This is behavior God hates. Proverbs 6:16-19 speaks on this topic:

> These six things doth the Lord hate: yea, seven are an abomination unto him: a proud look, a lying tongue, and hands that shed innocent blood, An heart that deviseth wicked imaginations, feet that be swift in running to mischief, a false witness that

speaketh lies, and he that soweth discord among brethren.

Gossipers possess a lying tongue and their gossip is sure to shed innocent blood along the way. Not every rumor they spread is true. And continuing to be the mouthpiece that spreads such poison could destroy people. Because "death and life are in the power of the tongue: and they that love it shall eat the fruit thereof" (18:21). The people quick and eager to listen to gossip are as guilty as the gossiper. Most often they will spread the gossip they've heard and may add a little bit to what they've heard, if they feel it will add more excitement to the story. They would never spread the truth with as much enthusiasm.

The gossiper is a foolish person: "A fool's lips enter into contention, and his mouth calleth for strokes. A fool's mouth is his destruction, and his lips are the snare of his soul" (vv. 6-7). The gossiper is forever running his mouth about someone else's business. Scripture labels gossipers "fools." Their lips are traps. Their mouths bring nothing but death, including their own. Their souls are imprisoned by darkness. Gossipers and liars will reap what they sow: "A false witness shall not be unpunished, and he that speaketh lies shall not escape" (19:5).

The Word of God cautions us against fraternizing with folks who spread gossip and slander their neighbors: "He that goeth about as a talebearer revealeth secrets: therefore meddle not with him that flattereth with his lips" (20:19). Gossipers and liars have chosen to go the way that seems right to them, but as believers we must do everything we can to uplift one another and to live peaceably with others.

God keeps reminding us to stay away from tearing down souls with our tongues. Psalm 34:13 makes the following pleas: "Keep thy tongue from evil, and thy lips from speaking guile." Gossipers and liars are numerous in the land. Lives are torn apart every day because of them. We have to pray for God's protection against those evil spirits that possess the tongue, causing it to speak death. Gossip and lies hurt everyone involved.

Our charge is this: "Let no corrupt communication proceed out of your mouth, but that which is good to the use of edifying, that it may minister grace unto the hearers" (Eph. 4:29). Anything that tries to teach otherwise is a lie. We should run from gossip and lies as fast as our feet can carry us. Liars and gossipers speak death. They belong to the father of lies. Eternal death has its claws embedded in the liar, the gossiper, and the audience whose ears are burning to hear the poison. Wouldn't you rather be a person who speaks life and be around the same?

Sexual Immorality
Sex is glorified: on billboards, on television, in the movies, in magazines, in novels, in music—everywhere. It is little wonder why sex outside of marriage has become so widely accepted as normal. Marriage has become an afterthought. Divorce is commonplace. Being faithful to one's spouse has lost its luster. All of this is because sin has blinded people. Darkness, to them, is more appealing.

The Word of God says sex outside the marriage of a man and a woman is sin (Heb. 13:4). Human beings, on the other hand, say that is a lie. Any sin a person engages in is usually the one he does not believe is a sin. What I am saying is this:

if the Bible says a particular thing is a sin, and the person is engaging in what the Bible deems a sin, then he or she will either twist the scripture around to mean something else or label it a flat-out lie. Again, the prince of the power of the air is using his power to deceive us into believing lies over truths and to view truths as lies.

The Bible addresses the sin of sexual immorality, so let's explore what it has to say. In Chapter 2, I spoke about the sin of homosexuality. I will touch on it again here, because I want to make it clear that homosexuality falls under the sin of sexual immorality. It is a sin of the flesh. Again, God loves the homosexual but hates the sin. I know, for some, it hurts to hear that something they feel to be natural is in fact unnatural. It's difficult to hear the truth, but for the sake of eternal life, the truth has to be told. The truth is, we must love each other and lift each other up in prayer. Hating others because they sin differently is unwise. It is what hypocrites do. We are all human beings who have to fight against falling into the trap of sin. We have to be each other's keeper, correcting one another and loving one another in a godly manner.

Before I speak further about homosexuality, it is important that I dispel the myth that Sodom and Gomorrah were destroyed only because of this specific sin. The full truth is so often lost in the telling of this story. Many of us have heard the story about Sodom and Gomorrah in the Bible and believe one part of it. It is true that some people choose the one sin they despise the most and blame the destruction of those cities on that particular sin. However, these cities were indeed filled with sin, with homosexuality being one of many sins committed there. God said, "... the cry of Sodom and Gomorrah is great … their sin is very grievous" (Gen. 18:20). Scripture also tells us "the men of Sodom were wicked and sinners before the Lord exceedingly" (13:13). Sadly the message is somehow skewed to include only one sin.

Genesis 19:4-9 tells of the wicked desires of both young and old men in the city of Sodom and how they wanted to know (sexually) the two angels who were staying the night in Lot's house, and how Lot offered his virgin daughters to the men to do as they please, and how the men burned in their desire for the angels. Lot said, "I pray you, brethren, do not so wickedly" (v. 7). In the New Testament, Jude, James's brother, also discussed the sin of homosexuality, as well as the sin of fornication, saying, "… Sodom and Gomorrah, and the cities about them in like manner, giving themselves over to fornication, and going after strange flesh, are set forth for an example, suffering the vengeance of eternal fire" (1:7). Sexual sin, like any other sin, leads to eternal damnation. That's the Word of God!

The entire truth of the story about Sodom and Gomorrah gets lost in the attribution of the destruction of those cities to homosexuality. The truth is that there were homosexuals in those wicked places, as the scripture attests. Another truth is that other sins were also great in the land. "What were Sodom's other sins?" you might ask. God laid out Sodom's sins in Ezekiel 16:49: "Behold, this was the iniquity of thy sister Sodom, pride, fulness of bread, and abundance of idleness was in her and in her daughters, neither did she strengthen the hand of the poor and needy." In that scripture God was comparing Jerusalem to Sodom and Samaria. Jerusalem, by the way, "wast corrupted more than they" (v. 47). The people of Jerusalem were corrupt in all their ways.

We can see as we study scripture that God would have spared Sodom and Gomorrah had he found a certain number of righteous individuals residing there. When God told Abraham of his plans to destroy Sodom, Abraham asked God, "Wilt thou also destroy the righteous with the wicked?" (Gen. 18:23). In verses 24 through 32, Abraham asks God how many righteous should be found in the land of Sodom for God not to destroy it. The number begins at fifty righteous men, but eventually goes down to ten. "I will not destroy it for ten's sake," said the Lord (v. 32). The end result: "Then the Lord rained upon Sodom and upon Gomorrah brimstone and fire from the Lord out of heaven" (19:24). God destroyed Sodom and Gomorrah because of sexual immorality, their pride in themselves for their accomplishments (they didn't give God the glory), slothfulness, gluttony, having no concern for the poor and needy, and arrogance.

God loves the sinner! God hates the sin! Rebellion against God leads to spiritual death. I want to drive home those truths. Choosing to have same-sex relationships is rebelling against God. Allow me to continue with biblical proof. God took the rib from Adam and made a woman and brought her to the man (Gen. 2:21-22). "Therefore shall a man leave his father and his mother, and shall cleave unto his wife: and they shall be one flesh" (v. 24). God did not make man for man or woman for woman, for them to know one another in a sexual way. Proverbs 18:22 notes, "Whoso findeth a wife findeth a good thing, and obtaineth favour of the Lord." We can draw from this scripture that the "whoso" refers to a man, because to God same-sex relationships are an "abomination" (Lev. 18:22; 20:13). God has dictated that marriage is between a man and a woman, saying they are "one flesh" (Matt. 19:5) and commanding that what He "hath joined together, let not man put asunder" (v. 6). Marriage between a man and a woman is approved by God. Concerning marriage, this is the final answer.

Nowhere in the Bible is it written that God looks favorably upon same-sex relationships or same-sex marriages. Teaching that marriage between two men or two women is acceptable is not sound doctrine. It is the teaching of the devil, because he knows if he can convince us to live in sin, we will belong to him.

The homosexual who burns in his or her desire for someone of the same sex, and considers his or her behavior as normal or natural, has accepted unsound doctrine as truth because he or she wants to satisfy the lust of the flesh. Too many men and women are turned away from truth if it goes against the desires of their flesh. And God, who is fed up with the rebellious ways of this generation, will turn men and women over to themselves:

> For this cause God gave them up unto vile affections: for even their women did change the natural use into that which is against nature: And likewise also the men, leaving the natural use of the woman, burned in their lust one toward another; men with men working that which is unseemly, and receiving in themselves that recompence of their error which was meet. And even as they did not like to retain God in their knowledge, God gave them over to a reprobate mind, to do those things which are not convenient.... (Rom. 1:26-28)

God is tired of our evil ways. Human beings have chosen to defy the Lord's truth, trusting instead in their own wisdom:

men and women "professing themselves to be wise, they became fools" (v. 22).

Same-sex relationships may be the most talked-about form of sexual immorality in this day, but ALL forms of sexual sin are equally destructive in God's eyes. Deceiving ourselves into believing that one sexual sin is worse than another does not change the fact that it all weighs heavily against the soul of the practitioner. Sexual sin covers a large territory. Galatians 5:19 gives us a quick glance at what sexual immorality is: "Now the works of the flesh are manifest, which are these; Adultery, fornication, uncleanness, lasciviousness...."

Adultery is just as much a sin as homosexuality, although it is not talked about nearly as much. It may be that people do not really view adultery as a sin. Adultery has a higher acceptance rate. "Everybody cheats," I've heard a lot of people say. Husbands leave their wives and families every day, many times for a younger woman who satisfies their lustful desires. A great number of women are also leaving their husbands for the chance to satisfy their own lustful appetites. These days, spouses are leaving their marriages at the drop of a dime, giving in to temptation because they do not desire to practice restraint. Staying in a marriage seems to be too much of a challenge that many men and women cannot, for one reason or another, live up to.

Most often, adultery is accepted as no big deal. The few people who consider adultery wrong are usually the committed spouses who are abandoned and the individuals who know and believe the gospel regarding adultery. The adulterer does not see that he is doing anything wrong. He carries on the adulterous affair because it feels good to him, and satisfying the flesh is what he loves. He has no concern that God does not approve. He is all about following his own heart.

When adultery takes place between a man and a woman, it is given some sort of pass because so many people accept it as a natural thing and justify adultery by saying something like, "Boys will be boys." This shows that we are less likely to hate a sin when we engage in that sin or view it as being "not as bad" as certain other sins. But God has spoken! "Thou shalt not commit adultery" (Exod. 20:14).

Adultery is not limited to physical engagement in an extra-marital affair. Jesus said, "whosoever looketh on a woman to lust after her hath committed adultery with her already in his heart" (Matt. 5:28). Lusting after someone, then, is also adultery. If you have any question about divorcing your spouse or what constitutes adultery, read what Jesus said:

> It hath been said, Whosoever shall put away his wife, let him give her a writing of divorcement: But I say unto you, That whosoever shall put away his wife, saving for the cause of fornication, causeth her to commit adultery: and whosever shall marry her that is divorced committeth adultery. (vv. 31-32)

In other words the only valid reason for divorcing a spouse is unfaithfulness. The Word goes a bit further, teaching also that "Whosoever shall put away his wife, except it be for for-nication, and shall marry another, committeth adultery: and whoso marrieth her which is put away doth commit adultery" (19:9). This means a man who divorces a wife who has not been unfaithful and marries another woman is guilty of the sin of adultery and so is the man who marries her. "For the woman which hath an husband is bound by the law to her husband so long as he liveth; but if the husband be dead, she is loosed from the law of her husband. So then if, while her husband liveth, she be married to another man, she shall be called an adulteress" (Rom. 7:2-3). The woman is allowed to remarry if her husband is dead. Marriage is meant to be a lifelong institution. But people's filthiness has caused them to make a mockery of marriage. Marriage has become a joke to people. God's truth, however, is forever binding.

Today countless people are living in adulterous marriages. If the divorce was because of fornication or if the subsequent marriage or marriages came after the death of the spouse(s), they do not fall under adultery. We may all have knowledge of people, ministers included, who have been married more than once, some even three or more times—and while the former spouse was yet alive. That is not to say second or third or fourth marriages are adulterous. It all depends on the reason the divorce took place. However, multiple divorces do speak to the lack of self-restraint in human beings. If men and women who have been ordained to preach the Word of God do not obey it, how much more will the lay person disobey God's Word?

God is as much against adultery as He is against any other sin of the flesh. It is sexually immoral, and that is the bottom line. Just because numerous people are living in adulterous marriages or stepping outside marriage does not make it any less a sin. Adulterers, like all other sinners, will meet their demise if they continue in their sin. Death is in the adulterer because he has rejected the gospel.

Breaking marriage vows tends to be a form of entertainment, pleasuring the flesh and spitting on the sanctity of lifelong commitment. In so doing, these people's souls are in trouble of damnation. The wise Solomon, David's son and Israel's king, said, "But whoso committeth adultery with a woman lacketh understanding: he that doeth it destroyeth his own soul" (Prov. 6:32). There! It has been said.

Next, fornication is a sexually immoral act between two people who are not married to one another. This sin also defiles the body. Paul said, "he that committeth fornication sinneth against his own body" (1 Cor. 6:18). Of all the acts of sexual immorality, fornication is likely by far the most widely practiced. It is viewed as harmless fun between two people. Sleeping with people before marriage is commonplace. Tens of millions of children are born out of wedlock, which means they were conceived in sin and were born into sin. The sinner believes that living together and carrying on sexual relationships with his girlfriend or her boyfriend is normal. It is called "playing the field," and the fornicator says, "Playing the field is normal. There is nothing wrong with it as long as it is consensual." Of course that is a lie. There IS something wrong with sleeping with anyone we are not married to. Satisfying the innermost lustful appetite works against the Word of God. It leads to death. "Nevertheless, to avoid fornication, let every man have his own wife, and let every woman have her own husband" (1 Cor. 7:2).

Temptations to accommodate the flesh surround us. Sex is incorporated into everything. Sex sells. We all know about online dating and escort services that offer more than casual dates. Available to the busy person are cell phone apps that help people connect for sexual encounters. Strip clubs, swingers' parties, and the like offer to satisfy one's darkest sexual fantasies. Prostitution and pornography are lucrative for the person willing to defile his or her body. Pornography is available both online and in local convenience stores. Some shops specifically cater to sexual fantasies. At one's convenience are phone numbers to call if he wants to tell his desires and fantasies to listening ears.

The devil plays on man's sexual desires and lusts, trapping them in dark places. He lures in the fornicator because he has done his homework. Satan's agents have led many sexually immoral persons to their deaths. People have met total strangers online, which led to meetings in person, which led to their demise. They place themselves in dangerous situations for the sake of experiencing sexual pleasure with strangers. Scarier still is that they risk losing their souls for eternity due to their appetite for sin.

Uncleanness and lasciviousness—lustful and lewd behavior—are enemies to the soul. When man's flesh is weak and his lusts are great, the devil is given a way in. The deceitful one knows our sinful desires and is able to tempt men and women who are not obedient to God's Word. Whatever we lust after, that is what the serpent will tempt us with. Giving in to temptations of the flesh has brought down many men and women, both believers and unbelievers. Sins of the flesh have trapped the foolish. Satisfying the lusts of the flesh has ensnared the polygamist and given incurable diseases to millions of men and women all over the world, young and old. Engaging in sexual immorality reveals the condition of sinners' hearts. Jesus explained this condition in Mark 7:20-23:

> That which cometh out of the man, that defileth
> the man. For from within, out of the heart of men,
> proceed evil thoughts, adulteries, fornications,

murders, Thefts, covetousness, wickedness, deceit, lasciviousness, an evil eye, blasphemy, pride,
foolishness: All these evil things come from within,
and defile the man.

Oh, how I can identify with that scripture! Like so many other
folk, I have to ask for forgiveness many times throughout
the day because in my heart I sin continuously. If you are
honest with yourself and are not one who deceives yourself
into believing you are without sin, you too will benefit from
seeking God's forgiveness. If anyone tells you that engaging
in sex outside of marriage is normal, distance yourself from
that person quickly. Such a person lacks understanding. God
expects us to flee from sin and from anyone advocating sin.

Temptation of the flesh is the devil's specialty. He does not
want us to come into the understanding of truth. Satan knows
that sin brings about death. Of course, to act on our lusts, we
have to have a willing heart and be willing to disobey God.
James, the son of Joseph and Mary, and Jesus's half-brother,
said, "But every man is tempted, when he is drawn away of
his own lust, and enticed. Then when lust hath conceived, it
bringeth forth sin: and sin, when it is finished, bringeth forth
death" (James 1:14-15).

Engaging in sexual immorality is natural to unbelievers
who reason in their own minds and rely on their own wisdom
to think that God would not have created so many people if
He wanted them to be with just one person. Leave it up to
man to twist God's Word to make it fit his own fleshy desires.
Nothing but death comes from fulfilling the desires of our
sinful flesh. Peter, Jesus's disciple, wrote, "Dearly beloved, I
beseech you as strangers and pilgrims, abstain from fleshly

lusts, which war against the soul" (1 Peter 2:11). And Paul said, "Know ye not that the unrighteous shall not inherit the kingdom of God? Be not deceived: neither fornicators ... nor abusers of themselves with mankind ... shall inherit the kingdom of God" (1 Cor. 6:9-10). Living a clean, holy lifestyle is required for entrance into the kingdom of God.

Disobedience and Unbelief

Anyone who forsakes the Word of God and chooses to live by his own truth sins against God. Disobedience is our refusal to adhere to God's commandments. Disregarding His commandments is the reason our prayers go unanswered. It is the cause of our troubles and suffering. The disobedient have nothing in common with God, but profess they do. The gospel reports, "They profess that they know God; but in works they deny him, being abominable, and disobedient, and unto every good work reprobate" (Titus 1:16). The works of a person will always reveal whom he serves. The unbeliever and the disobedient serve the devil.

When we choose to make the Word of God a lie, we become children of the devil. Satan is better able to use us to accomplish his deadly master plan in our separation from God. Recall Ephesians 2:2, and how it tells us about the spirit of evil that dwells inside us when we walk "according to the course of this world, according to the prince of the power of the air, the spirit that now worketh in the children of disobedience."

The devil's spirit is in those who willingly disobey God. Satan is their father. Separation from God puts us in the dark, where we cannot distinguish between lies and truths. So we are more prone to travel down roads that lead to our destruction. We can say we love God all we want, but if we are not doing the will of God, we do not love Him but rather Satan, who is sin. Jesus said, "If ye love me, keep my commandments" (John 14:15).

Don't be deceived by people who are running around living for the world, according to the world, and doing everything God commanded them not to do. They can tell you they are children of God all they want, but do not be fooled. Their disobedience to God will prove whose children they are. Scripture teaches, "Ye are of your father the devil, and the lusts of your father ye will do" (John 8:44). People who do and say all manners of evil are not of God. A person's actions will always reveal whom that individual serves. They can deny it. They can call it something different. They can twist the scripture to try to justify their evil, but those who study and adhere to the gospel of truth will not be tricked by the devil's lies.

Disobedience is rebellion. "For rebellion is as the sin of witchcraft, and stubbornness is as iniquity and idolatry" (1 Sam. 15:23). Rebellion turns God's hand against us. Samuel taught "if ye will not obey the voice of the LORD, but rebel against the commandment of the LORD, then shall the hand of the LORD be against you, as it was against your fathers" (12:15). Rebelling against God makes us targets of the devil's fiery darts also. The Bible warns, "if ye refuse and rebel, ye shall be devoured with the sword: for the mouth of the LORD hath spoken it" (Isa. 1:20). On the other hand God's Word also promises, "If ye be willing and obedient, ye shall eat the good of the land" (v. 19). Which would you prefer?

On another level of death, unbelief is found. Jesus spoke to the unbeliever, who is unable to hear the truth:

If God were your Father, ye would love me: for I proceeded forth and came from God; neither came I of myself, but he sent me. Why do ye not understand my speech? even because ye cannot hear my word.... And because I tell you the truth, ye believe me not. Which of you convinceth me of sin? And if I say the truth, why do ye not believe me? He that is of God heareth God's words: ye therefore hear them not, because ye are not of God (John 8:42-43, 45-47).

Simply put, unbelievers are not of God. The truth does not reside in them. Their hearts are turned away from God. Their minds are in the world. Their belief and trust are in their own way. In their unbelief they can live without restrictions. Believing the Word of God would mean they would have to be responsible, have restraint, and be held accountable by God. Unbelievers engage in whatever behavior satisfies their flesh. Believing in God would actually give them a conscience so that they could self-correct, which is something they desire not.

There are some who say, "I believe in God, but I do not believe in the Bible because it was written by men." They say that God couldn't have written such things that are in the Bible. The apostle Paul wrote the truth in his letter to Timothy, which was penned from the confines of Paul's prison cell. He said, "All scripture is given by inspiration of God, and is profitable for doctrine, for reproof, for correction, for instruction in righteousness: That the man of God may be perfect, thoroughly furnished unto all good works" (2 Tim. 3:16-17). The Word of God is intended to give order and light to a chaotic and sinful world. We are to use it to encourage one another to

follow the straight path. The Word of God is meant for healing
the ills of the world and sin-sick man. But the unbeliever will
hear none of it. His ways are destruction.

Unbelievers teach false doctrine. They say that Jesus was
just another man and should not be worshipped, that He is
separate from God. It reminds me of the day I was convers-
ing with a woman I'd been familiar with since childhood. We
stood under a tree in the middle of our hometown, talking
and laughing. We then began to talk about God, because I'm
always excited to talk about Him and to spread His truth. The
woman shared a story of her journey from the Christian faith
to another faith. She'd recently left Christianity due to her
being unable to "tolerate the preacher lying to the congregation anymore." She said Christian churches teach congrega-
tions to worship Jesus, but they should be teaching them to
worship Jehovah instead.

The lady sounded passionate about what she now believed
to be the truth—that Jesus was just another man. She said
the Christian church has it all wrong. My heart sank. I knew
the devil had deceived her. I allowed her to walk away without shedding some light on the false belief, because I did not
want to tell her she was wrong for her beliefs. I felt that she
wouldn't get the gospel of truth because I believed she did
not want someone telling her anything other than what she
now accepted as truth. Walking away from that conversation, I beat myself up for missing the opportunity to share the
gospel of Christ with her, to tell her Jesus Christ is the only
way we can enter the kingdom of God. For whatever reason,
though, my mouth could not utter any of those words. Then
she was gone. And there I was, with many thoughts running
through my head and hoping that God wouldn't hold against

me my failure to spread the gospel of truth to that woman on that day under that tree in the middle of town.

I don't know why I could not say the words: "But Jesus is not just a man. He is the One we must go through to get to God." So I will tell you, and hopefully you will hear the truth. Scripture teaches, "In the beginning was the Word, and the Word was with God, and the Word was God. The same was in the beginning with God" (John 1:1-2). Jesus is the Living Word. And Jesus said, "I am the way, the truth, and the life: no man cometh unto the Father, but by me" (14:6). There is no other way to enter into the kingdom but through the Son. Further Jesus said, "ye believe in God, believe also in me" (v. 1). If we do not believe in Jesus, we do not believe in the Word, and if we do not believe in the Word, we do not believe in Jesus or the Holy Spirit who bears witness of Him, or in God, who sent them. Believing in one and not the others makes us unbelievers. Unbelievers abide in lies and are of the devil.

To avoid running into the same dead end as the unbeliever, the believer must not allow himself to be turned away from truth. The consequence of disobedience and unbelief is a sentence to the bottomless pit. Once we are in hell, there is no escape. Jesus asked, "Ye serpents, ye generation of vipers, how can ye escape the damnation of hell? (Matt. 23:33). That is the question Jesus is still asking us, this current evil generation. Are we ready to listen?

Right now God will not hear us due to our disobedience and unbelief. How do we know this? The scripture tells us, of course: "Behold, the LORD's hand is not shortened, that it cannot save; neither his ear heavy, that it cannot hear: But your iniquities have separated between you and your God, and your sins have hid his face from you, that he will not hear" (Isa. 59:1-2).

God is ready to forgive us and to heal the world. God's love is unconditional, but for Him to answer our cries for help, we are required to obey His Word. You ask, "When will God heal our land, and what must we do?" Here is the answer: "If my people, which are called by my name, shall humble themselves, and pray, and seek my face, and turn from their wicked ways; then will I hear from heaven, and will forgive their sin, and will heal their land" (2 Chron. 7:14).

9
Fear: Satan's Greatest Tactic

FEAR IS PERHAPS Satan's greatest tactic for keeping his kingdom afloat. The ol' sneaky serpent has used fear to keep his tradition of hate, bondage, oppression, and injustice thriving. The devil knows that if he can silence the voices of mankind, he can go about killing, stealing, and destroying. That is why the prince of the power of the air tries everything in his power to get into the heads of those who doubt God. If someone doubts God, he gives power to the enemy. And the enemy then takes that power and uses various scenarios to cripple us, to make us ill, and to keep us from rising to our full potential.

Fear does not come from God: "For God hath not given us the spirit of fear; but of power, and of love, and of a sound mind" (2 Tim. 1:7). Scripture, then, reassures us in case we forget. We are blessed with the spirit of power. That means if we want to move obstacles out of our way, we can. If we want to triumph over the enemy, we have that power. And

the power that God gives us is more than enough to render powerless anything that threatens to defeat us. That
includes the devil and his agents, who only have the power
we give them. So why do we walk in fear? Why is it that
we allow Satan and his agents to crush us? You've heard it
before: when we sin, we separate ourselves from God, and
He from us—not His love, but His power and favor. When we
are marred by sin, we no longer have access to the power
that God has blessed us with.

Fear paralyzes and immobilizes the majority of us. Because
of fear we exist within our self-constructed, four-wall prison
where we have no sense of power. What do we fear? We fear
failure, standing up for what is right, being alone or abandoned, the unknown, being disliked or rejected, etc. We fear
achievement because of how others might criticize us. We fear
others—people in high positions, the bully, the loudmouth,
those who have a large following, the criminal, and the list
goes on—and what they may do to us. It's fear, fear, fear, and
more fear. We give fear so much power. We have elevated our
fears above God. We may not say it, but we live like it. Fear is
the master of those who cannot see God.

Fear comes from a place of sin and disobedience. In the
Garden of Eden, Adam and Eve hid themselves because, after
they disobeyed God's command, they became fearful (Gen.
3:8; 10). Today we have our own wicked ways to thank for
fear. When we engage in sin, doing the very things God has
instructed us not to do, we cannot hear God's voice. And that
puts us in an unsafe place where we feel all alone and unpro-
tected. In the valley of the shadow of death that is this world,
we find ourselves in situations that create great terror and
anxiety.

The world today is filled with fear. People are always talking about fearing one thing and another. When we lack faith in God's power, fear becomes our god, ruling our lives and denying us the peace to live freely. A major problem is that we are discounting God's power to reign supreme in our lives. Instead we give more credit to the enemy, thereby handing him the steering wheel. We become like small boats, shaken to and fro in violent winds when we hand over control of our lives to the devil. If we are giving the enemy credit for being more powerful than the God in us, then fear dictates how we live.

Fear is a god in and of itself. Its roots are deeply planted in the tricks and trades of the devil. Satan controls the power of the air, getting into our thoughts and tricking us into believing that we have to be afraid. We become afraid of people who are different than we are because the devil has fooled us into believing that differences are dangerous. But we are not supposed to walk around in fear. Taking our eyes off God, and getting caught up in the world and its endless lies, diminishes our God-given power. If we are incapable of seeing past this world, we make everything about this world. Then the world overwhelms us and causes us to be anxious and fearful and vulnerable. God is screaming out to us that we shouldn't fear and that He has given us courage. All we have to do is trust that the Lord is our rock and shield.

Fear is a spirit from the devil. Fear is a spirit that binds the sinful and the faithless. It is a way of life for those who give in to it. Walking in fear makes us useless to God. How can we do His will if we are full of fear? How can God be glorified when the world looks at us and sees cowards? Lack of courage makes us slaves to the world. But if we truly believe that God is all-powerful, all-knowing, and in all places, and that He is able to protect us from evil and deliver us out of the hands of the enemy, then we can go about our daily lives, feeling completely safe and knowing we have the power to stand up for ourselves and for the weak. If we truly believe, then we can go anywhere and know that the hand of God is our strength, and that He will work everything out for our good (Rom. 8:28).

Having faith is necessary to live the life God wants us to live. Living in fear is not what He wants for us. How can God, who is all-powerful, have children who are cowards? He cannot. God's children are courageous. They shut down fear before it has time to fester. God's children are powerful. Satan's children have a false sense of power but are cowards who get their power from their wealth, connections, and status. The world gives their own what amounts to the illusion of power. To them, however, their power is real. The power that God gives His children is present even in the eye of the storm. That's real and true power.

Fear is Satan's way of controlling generation after generation of lost souls. Fear renders our every idea, every decision, every plan worthless. One of the devil's own personal fears is that we will break free from fear. He fears God, and so when we tap into the power God has given us, the devil becomes powerless. The devil is the father of cowardice—he knows that cowards cannot inherit the kingdom of heaven. Satan's days are numbered, and he wants fear to destroy us. Breaking the chains of fear means that we must give God complete control over our lives, trusting totally in Him.

Breaking the chains of fear also increases our potential for God. We blossom in the absence of fear, and we are free to create wonderful things. We can live life without limits, without being deterred by others' opinions of us. Unbound from fear, we can move forward in power and not give up any of our power to anyone ever again. Our courage and belief will allow us to rise above what the enemy thinks we deserve. When we are free of fear, we don't sit by and wait on others to hand us anything. Satan's earthly gatekeepers can either approve or deny us, but it will not stop us from walking in the favor of God. Releasing fear is like taking a deep breath of fresh air. It is living the wonderful life we were meant to live without falling in love with the world, because that would open us up to fear all over again. When we say no to fear, we become courageous soldiers of God, able to change the world for the better, deny unfairness, and stand up for the best interests of ALL people.

When we say no to fear, we can advance. A million people can be against us, and we will face them, head-on, and render them powerless. We will walk through the fire and not be burned. The enemy's trap will be obvious to us when we walk in the power of the Lord. In the face of our power, defeat will hide its face. Giving up will be comedy to us. We know that if we walk upright and stand courageously, we are covered by our Creator. Our faith in God will not allow the enemy to shame us. The enemy will become the footstool to the righteous children of God. There is work to do if we are to walk in power and make our enemies our footstools. We have to totally surrender to God.

We have to be courageous enough to stand up for the oppressed, the poor, and the unjustly accused. We are required by God to do so. We have to stand up against injustice as much as we have to stand up against crime. Bad things happen because cowards stand around, too afraid to speak up against perpetrators. The coward does not want to get involved, and so bad things continue to happen. "Good" people do not stand around and allow injustice to go on. "Good" people do not sit back and allow innocent people to be unjustly treated. "Good" people stand up to the bad guy whether it causes them discomfort or not. Murders and other crimes will never cease if "good" people do not take a stand and say "No more!"

Threats of loss scare "good" people into becoming part of the problem—the problem being silence. If a person is not standing up for what is right and what pleases God, he is not a "good" person but a coward who is part of the bad person's camp. There is no such thing as a "good" person standing around and allowing innocent people to be cheated, lied to, tricked, or injured in any way. The devil tells the lie that there are many "good" people, but those "good" people are part of the problem, because they remain silent and tuck their tails between their legs and walk away in order to avoid criticism from the devil's agents and gatekeepers. A part of walking in power and being courageous is being willing to face harsh criticism, name-calling, and loss (e.g., loss of career, loss of finances, loss of family and friends). "If God be for us, who can be against us?" (Rom. 8:31). Whatever we lose in our fight to make the lives of all people bearable and free from oppression, God will restore to us—and His restoration will be more than generous.

How many times have we heard of people turning a blind eye to crime? We somehow convince ourselves that it's better not to get involved, that it's in our best interest to keep our mouths shut. We do this to avoid getting ourselves involved in anything that might come back to harm us. In actuality, when we allow bad things to happen to innocent people, we will one day find ourselves in a similar situation. Turning a blind eye may postpone our run-in with the bad guy, but crime will finally catch up with us too. We cannot continue to allow the innocent to be ambushed. We have to speak out, because it's the only thing that's going to make this world a better and safer place to live. If the so-called good and innocent among us don't band together, the bad will keep winning. One thing bad people do is join other bad people in their pursuit of destruction. This is how their reign of terror begins. The bad reign supreme—only because the "good" are too fearful. Their fear displeases God. Fear will be their destruction.

Fear can sneak up on us and catch hold of us without warning. When we are attacked by the enemy, the experience can leave us fearful of ever stepping out of our comfort zone. It can leave us unwilling to change our lives for the better. When fear overwhelms us, we abandon our goals and see our dreams as unattainable. When the enemy begins looking at us, we fear going out into the world, because whatever the enemy says about us may prove to be too embarrassing to us, and we don't want to feel the discomfort of having society boycott us, pass around petitions to silence us, treat us with contempt, or bring harm to us. We convince ourselves that it's much easier to hide away and wrap ourselves in the blanket of mediocrity than to face being criticized, booed, called names, talked about, and hated.

In the mid to late 1990s, as I stood in the midst of my enemies, I feared them with a fear I had never before experienced. Their words and harsh criticism crushed me. I had no heart, no courage. All I could do in their presence was hang my head and cry. When the fear grew to the point that I felt completely overwhelmed, I tried to make myself less visible. I accepted a life of mediocrity. At least in the rut I'd resigned myself to,

I didn't have to worry much about the devil's chosen people tearing me down and embarrassing me with lies that looked like truths to the unlearned. With my entire being I gave in to that fear, and it caused me anxiety, heartache, regret, and despair. I wandered in the wilderness of fear and embarrassment for many years.

Fear crippled me emotionally and bound me to the depths of darkness. Because of fear I resigned myself to that place where nothing good could possibly happen in my life. I had projected into the universe a negative energy that wilted everything around me. More than ten years passed before I began to work my way out of that dark hole. In those ten years, and for many years after, I suffered from severe anxiety. I didn't want to leave the house, and if I had been financially secure, I would not have left the house. But I was poor and had to work so that I could eat. But I didn't go far. I didn't aim high. Fear still held me down. I can tell you that living in fear is a horrible existence and it glorifies the devil.

In my eyes those employed by the devil to destroy me became larger-than-life creatures and took on almost divine powers—a deception that blinded me to the truth for many years. I saw my late twenties and all my thirties pass me by as I lived in slow motion. It seemed at the time like many lifetimes had passed me by. As I began to study the Bible and spend time with God, developing a stronger bond with Him, the fear and anxiety started to fade out of my life. The truth became clearer to me. The evil that had come to destroy me, to possess my soul, to compel me to worship at its feet, to grovel before Satan, and to convince me that my life was worthless and my future doomed, turned out to be no more powerful than I allowed it to be.

Sure, the enemy and his army can do some damage in our lives. They can even take our lives. However, they are incapable of staking claim to our spirit without our consent. Jesus commanded, "fear not them which kill the body, but are not able to kill the soul" (Matt. 10:28). For many years I existed under a heavy cloud of fear. I could not hear God speaking to me, telling me to trust in Him. Here it is now, over two decades later, and I am finally listening to Him. I settled for the crumbs that fell from the enemy's table because I lived in fear of people who do not possess the power to touch me beyond this earthly life. How much wasted time I spent living under that cloud when all I had to do was have a little faith in the Almighty!

Today I have no problem admitting that I lived in fear. There is no need for anyone to be ashamed of having once lived in fear. Everyone has at some point in his or her life lived in fear. We are not immune to fear, especially if we don't understand that fear is the devil's way of enslaving us. The devil has deceived us all. He uses whatever scheme he can to persuade us that we have a reason to live in fear. If he can deceive us into believing that we deserve to live in fear, then we become slaves to thugs, criminals, unruly children, mean-spirited people, and every type of bully we can ever imagine. We fear they will attack us, rob us, trap us, lie about us, and/or kill us.

Bullies—who come in three-piece, designer suits as well as pants sagging below the waist—sense our fear and feed off it, thereby increasing their strength and power. We do whatever we can to avoid or appease them. We seek to, perhaps, gain their approval. In bowing to the enemy—the "powerful" and "influential" enemy (who comes in all nationalities, skin types, races, and economic backgrounds)—we make the choice to serve the devil and live under the thumb of those who choose to work for him. We trade in the clothing of a courageous soldier for the rags and ways of a coward.

Are you living in fear today? What is your greatest fear? Whatever your fears may be and however strong they seem to be, the way to banish that fearful spirit is to earnestly talk about it with God in prayer, to study the His Word, and to carry the Word in your heart.

Know that God has given us power over our fears. God is the only being we should fear. He tells us why we should fear Him. Going back to Matthew 10:28: "... but rather fear him which is able to destroy both soul and body in hell." Solomon said, "The fear of the Lord is the beginning of wisdom: and the knowledge of the holy is understanding" (Prov. 9:10). Wisdom and knowledge ensure we are always aware that the Lord protects us because He cares for us, and that the Holy Spirit guides us away from evil. Fearing God makes us want to walk in righteousness. We are mindful of what is right and what is good, and we live accordingly. Our fear of the Lord is to keep us in check, to have us love and do right by one another. God's will is that our hands remain free of mischief and open and extended to our brothers and sisters.

God has no use for the fearful, who are also called cowards. There is no place for them in God's kingdom. "But the fearful ... shall have their part in the lake which burneth with fire and brimstone: which is the second death" (Rev. 21:8). The fearful (the cowards) will have given in to the world and lived by the world and will have existed without fear of the Lord. The fearful will have allowed being called a "snitch" or a "troublemaker" or being bullied to keep them from fighting the good fight.

Speaking of the word "snitch," this word is used by cowards to keep others from interfering with their breaking the law and bringing harm to their neighbors. It is a small, one-syllable word that keeps millions from doing the right thing. It is the same small word that will keep the fearful from gaining eternal life. A lawbreaking coward is often able to keep up his criminal behavior because of the power of that little word. The word has such negative connotation that nobody ever wants to be called a snitch. However, if we are to defeat the criminal, we have to turn him in. We have to say something when they do wrong. It is the right thing to do, and it will please God. We have to replace cowardice, which is the product of fear and unbelief, with faith. With faith we can push past our fears: "But without faith it is impossible to please him: for he that cometh to God must believe that he is, and that he is a rewarder of them that diligently seek him" (Heb. 11:6). Do not allow words to keep you from doing the right thing.

One of my favorite scriptures in the Bible comes from the book of Matthew:

> But the ship was now in the midst of the sea, tossed with waves: for the wind was contrary. And in the fourth watch of the night Jesus went unto them, walking on the sea. And when the disciples saw him walking on the sea, they were troubled, saying, It is a spirit; and they cried out for fear. But straightway Jesus spake unto them, saying, Be of good cheer; it is I; be not afraid. (14:24-27)

God is saying to us, "Cheer up, My children! Don't be afraid. I, your Creator, am with you." How comforting is it to know that we who believe in God and do His will are under His protection! Taking our eyes off God and focusing on the fears of the world is like being lured into a trap. Fear is the devil's tool. God didn't give it to us, so why would we take hold of it?

Let me conclude this chapter with some words of wisdom and encouragement regarding what is available to those who have faith in God. "The fear of man bringeth a snare: but whoso putteth his trust in the LORD shall be safe" (Prov. 29:25). You read that correctly: fear is a trap! The second part offers powerful reassurance that should comfort the soul: when we trust in God, we will be safe. Just think of it like this: God is our bodyguard. Nothing can harm us when we have faith in Him. God is encouraging all of us to walk in power and rest in His arms.

Faith in God is our saving grace. Faith stomps out fear and is our safety net. "If ye have faith as a grain of mustard seed, ye shall say unto this mountain, Remove hence to yonder place; and it shall remove; and nothing shall be impossible unto you" (Matt. 17:20). But to gain that level of power, we have to pray and fast: "Howbeit this kind goeth not out but by prayer and fasting" (v. 21). What is your mountain—your biggest obstacle? Are you willing to pray and fast? If so, nothing shall be impossible for you. Do you want the kind of power that moves mountains? Then do as God commands and fear not!

10

The Mind: Satan's Favorite Playground

SOME THINGS CANNOT be repeated often enough. In this book I have used a couple scriptures in part or whole multiple times. I do that because they are appropriate and because they speak to the situation at hand. One such scripture I've used more than once is this: "For God hath not given us the spirit of fear; but of power, and of love, and of a sound mind" (2 Tim. 1:7). That one verse addresses many areas. Most importantly it should give us hope, knowing that God has equipped us with power to move mountains, with love to overcome evil, and with mental and spiritual strength to combat the devil's devices that threaten to steal our sanity. God furnished us with these tools because He knows what we are up against in the devil's world—the forces of evil that are both evident and hidden.

In Chapter 9 we covered how the prince of darkness tries to inject fear into our spirits. The Creator, who is all-powerful, bestowed upon us His power. That power is enough to get us through this sin-filled and sin-sick world. The power God gave to us is sufficient to rule over the evil forces of this present world. Walking around feeling powerless magnifies the power of the devil. That means we have no faith in the power God has given us; being fearful means that in our lives, we have downgraded God to the status of a liar. Scripture says, "God is not a man, that he should lie; neither the son of man, that he should repent: hath he said, and shall he not do it? or hath he spoken, and shall he not make it good?" (Num. 23:19). Remember this: God is not a liar. Human beings who walk around this earth feeling powerless and fearful are not in God; neither is God in them. Possessing a spirit of fear means that we are sons and daughters of the world. For us to be able to tap into His power, we must believe the gospel that tells us God has given us power. Fear comes only from the ruler of this world—the devil. Remember this also: God's children are powerful and will use that power to uplift and to speak life into others.

God bestowed upon us the spirit of love. "Why did God give us the spirit of love?" you may ask. Because "God is love" (1 John 4:8). Anything outside of love—meaning hate—is not of God. His Word tells us this: "He that loveth not knoweth not God" (v. 8). Do not be fooled into believing that hate is love or concern or compassion or caring. It is not. It is evil and has no concern. It does not show compassion, only animosity. It is not caring, only careless and selfish. And do not be fooled by hate that disguises itself as love. The children of God know what love is and can't confuse love with hate. Hate causes harm and "love worketh no ill to his neighbor: therefore love is the fulfilling of the law" (Rom. 13:10). The truth about love (charity) is this:

Charity suffereth long, and is kind; charity envieth not; charity vaunteth not itself, is not puffed up, Doth not behave itself unseemly, seeketh not her own, is not easily provoked, thinketh no evil; Rejoiceth not in iniquity, but rejoiceth in the truth; Beareth all things, believeth all things, hopeth all things, endureth all things. Charity never faileth.... (1 Cor. 13:4-8)

Then there is the mind. God has given each of us a sound mind. It should be enough just to know that the all-knowing and all-powerful God has given us a sound mind and that He has made us in His image. That is what God has told us. Unfortunately God's Word is not enough for a large number of us.

In this present day the mind seems to be so fragile and wracked with worries, mental illnesses, doubt, overthinking, evil thoughts, and confusion. What corrupts the mind? Why, if God has given us a sound mind, would our minds be so weak as to persuade us to believe things that are not real? To believe lies? Why do people suffer crippling mental anguish? What causes our minds to be so weak, so fragile, and so susceptible to caving in to hallucination and fantasy? If God has given us sound minds, why do we live in despair and our own mental prisons? There are so many questions that appear to have no answers. But rest assured that there are answers to all the above questions.

The mind is impressionable. Yes—very much so! When we are children, our minds are shaped by our environment. Children take everything in. Whatever we are taught, the things we experience, and what we see in our early years become a part of our makeup. Those early teachings follow us into adulthood. When we become adults, our minds are largely products of our upbringing. If we are taught as children to be critical of people who don't look like us, we will, to some degree or other, continue to be critical of those same differences as adults. Also, it has been proven that children who were abused oftentimes become abusers themselves. Again, they learn from their experiences.

Children who are taught to value the ways of the world are likely to live according to the world in their adulthood. If children are given everything, they will probably want everything as adults. If they get their way as children, they will more than likely grow up with a sense of entitlement. Unloved, neglected, and abandoned children will probably grow up feeling inferior and empty, and have contempt for their peers who seem to have everything at their disposal. People have killed for that very reason. With children who grow up not being held accountable, it is highly unlikely they will grow into adults who take responsibility for their actions. Of course there are some exceptions to all of this.

Because children grow up one way, this does not, however, always mean they remain stuck that way throughout their lives. I am not saying this is a one-size-fits-all theory. What I am saying is that there's a high likelihood of a child's environment shaping his mind. It's not always true that a child will become his upbringing or that as an adult he will exhibit the same behaviors he learned as a child. I am not saying he or she will live out their upbringing permanently. It is possible that an adult with childhood issues can work through and release those issues to live a life that pleases God. All is not lost, as the mental health "experts" and other people of the world would have us believe when it comes to a "bad" childhood dictating the outcome of adulthood. It varies according to the individual. Some people want to do better and they do in fact do better, whereas others want to use their "undesirable" upbringing as an excuse not to change for the better.

Some children are given everything, including their parents' love and affection, and they later live lawless lifestyles. Again, it is an individual thing. Training children in the ways of God, teaching them through scripture, and modeling godly behavior will go a long way to improve his or her life. The adults in a child's life are responsible for rearing him or her in the ways of God. Training includes punishing the unruly child. If parents love their children, they will correct them: "He that spareth his rod hateth his son: but he that loveth him chasteneth him betimes" (Prov. 13:24). Parents cannot leave it to others their children encounter along the way to train them (including the church). Parents should be the role models—with Jesus as the ultimate role model.

Not every person is a believer in the ways of God. Some will teach children the opposite of the gospel of Jesus Christ. Many will teach children the evils that they believe, and those evils will bring dishonor to the adults who raised them. "The rod and reproof give wisdom: but a child left to himself bringeth his mother to shame" (29:15). That scripture does not give parents the license to abuse the child or to cut him down with harsh words, but to teach him in a loving and caring manner that evil behavior is not acceptable. Discipline is given because the parent loves the child and wants the best for her. Training and correcting a child according to the gospel will contribute to the shaping of his adult mind.

Based on what we allow into our minds as adults, we become either positive or negative, optimistic or pessimistic, healthy or ill, secure or insecure, free in Christ or paralyzed with fear and anxiety. Allowing trash into our minds, trashes our minds. When we dwell on sinful things, our minds will eventually blur the line between sin and righteousness. The carnal mind will first deceive us into believing that if our minds can conceive something, then it must be okay to engage in whatever it is. Or we could know our thoughts are wrong, but because we spend so much time entertaining them, those thoughts sooner or later push us into committing the act anyway. We risk satisfying the flesh when we give power to sinful thoughts.

Romans 8:5-6 explains the difference between the carnal mind and the spiritual mind: "For they that are after the flesh do mind the things of the flesh; but they that are after the Spirit the things of the Spirit. For to be carnally minded is death; but to be spiritually minded is life and peace." We see that it is beneficial to be spiritually minded. In the spiritually minded is life and peace. A carnal mind works to our detriment. Existing in a carnal mind is death. The scripture tells us why: "Because the carnal mind is enmity against God: for it is not subject to the law of God, neither indeed can be" (v. 7). When our minds are set on engaging in behaviors that please our flesh and the people of the world, then our minds are at the mercy of the enemy. That means our minds become extremely fragile and easily breakable.

Satan attacks the carnal mind. To understand this, we must understand Satan's position as the god of this world, knowing that human beings who do not believe in God will put up no resistance. Do you remember the scripture about those who are lost? The second book of Corinthians tells us that "the god of this world hath blinded the minds of them which believe not" (4:4). Satan is against the gospel of truth because it teaches us that he has been defeated. If people accept the gospel, then his power is no more. For now, the devil reigns over the lost whose thoughts are carnal, those who walk according to the flesh.

Walking in the flesh glorifies and gives power to the devil. When our thoughts are in agreement with the world and the things of the world, we subject ourselves to all sorts of mental chaos. And when our minds are attacked, it is the god of this world—the devil himself—doing the attacking. After a time of filling ourselves with the lies of the devil, the power of our minds will ultimately suffer a breakdown, having no clarity, no concept of truth, no conscience. The Bible explains this: "Unto the pure all things are pure: but unto them that are defiled and unbelieving is nothing pure; but even their mind and con- science is defiled" (Titus 1:15).

The corrupt mind is no longer sound after it is blinded to the gospel of truth. The corrupt mind is perhaps the devil's favorite playground. Scripture states that "so do these also resist the truth: men of corrupt minds, reprobate concerning the faith" (2 Tim. 3:8). Resisting the truth is the fruit of the devil's children. When we possess a corrupt state of mind, the devil uses us to destroy each other.

The unsound mind is the mind that devours what is good and can no longer function in power and in truth. Everything runs together. Judgment is clouded. Lies turn into truths, and truths into lies. Corrupt minds turn illusions into realities. Sound advice is rejected. Diseases of the mind overtake us. We begin to hear things, to look in the mirror and see things that are not there, replacing the natural image with horrible images of ourselves. Trying to attain the unattainable image the devil has put into our now corrupt minds will lead to self-destruction. Corrupt minds are paranoid and unstable minds. We have to keep reminding ourselves that God has given us sound minds!

Our minds will eventually betray us if we go long enough focusing on what is happening in the world. Problems and worries will appear to the unfocused mind as immovable mountains. Years of living according to our carnal minds will take away our ability to think rationally. Our carnal minds are where debilitating mental torment comes to rest, because torment cannot find space in the sound mind. This is because the sound mind only has room for the things of God. God tells us that He "wilt keep him in perfect peace, whose mind is stayed on thee: because he trusteth in thee" (Isa. 26:3).

Too many of us live under the stresses of everyday life. We are on overload. To make matters worse, Satan forever plays mind games with us, telling us we are not good enough, not pretty enough, not smart enough, not strong enough, not deserving enough. He tells us the things of the world are more important than anything else, and that if we do not have them, we are nothing. He uses criticism and harsh words to tear us down and make us doubt God and ourselves, and who we are in relation to the world. What we hear remains stuck in our heads. Then we start to "fix" ourselves to prove we are not what other people say we are. But the fixes don't work, so we continue to search for more fixes. This desire for fixes soon turns into a lifelong journey of fruitless searching, putting our minds in a constant state of turmoil because we have focused on what the world says about how we should live, act, and be.

In our endless search to fix ourselves in hopes of gaining the world's approval, we forget about what God says is important. God tells us it is important that we nourish our spiritual being. God's instruction is this: "Set your affection on things above, not on things on the earth" (Col. 3:2). In thinking on the things of God, we put ourselves in a position of knowledge, where the world has no permission to tell us who we are and how we should live. When we finally hear the Word of God, we understand what the devil is trying to do. We become aware of the tactics the devil uses to attempt to steal our minds. A healthy mind is a strong mind, and a mind is made strong by holding on to God's truths. A mind bogged down in the mud of the world is a weak mind. A weak mind is our enemy.

To strengthen your mind and guard it against the wiles of the devil, who aims to mentally exhaust us to the point of throwing in the towel, study the scriptures listed below. Remember them. Believe them. Hold them in your heart.

- Finally, brethren, whatsoever things are true, whatsoever things are honest, whatsoever things are just, whatsoever things are pure, whatsoever things are lovely, whatsoever things are of good report; if there be any virtue, and if there be any praise, think on these things. (Phil. 4:8)
- Be careful for nothing; but in every thing by prayer and supplication with thanksgiving let your requests be made known unto God. And the peace of God, which passeth all understanding, shall keep your hearts and minds through Christ Jesus. (Phil. 4:6-7)
- For though we walk in the flesh, we do not war after the flesh: (For the weapons of our warfare are not carnal, but mighty through God to the pulling down of strong holds;) Casting down imaginations, and every

high thing that exalteth itself against the knowledge of God, and bringing into captivity every thought to the obedience of Christ.... (2 Cor. 10:3-5)

- And be not conformed to this world: but be ye transformed by the renewing of your mind, that ye may prove what is that good, and acceptable, and perfect, will of God. (Rom. 12:2)
- Trust in the LORD with all thine heart; and lean not unto thine own understanding. In all thy ways acknowledge him, and he shall direct thy paths. (Prov. 3:5-6)
- Wherefore gird up the loins of your mind, be sober, and hope to the end for the grace that is to be brought unto you at the revelation of Jesus Christ.... (1 Peter 1:13)
- Come unto me, all ye that labour and are heavy laden, and I will give you rest. (Matt. 11:28)
- I can do all things through Christ which strengtheneth me. (Phil. 4:13)
- ... with his stripes we are healed. (Isa. 53:5)

The gospel of our God will heal us. It will transform and renew our minds. The Word of God "is a lamp unto my feet, and a light unto my path" (Ps. 119:105). That is what God's Word is for us. It provides solutions to all our problems. We need not argue with anyone concerning God's instructions. All we have to do is point out His words. If people are intent on trying to prove the scriptures wrong or trying to get us to turn away from God's Word, we must walk away from those people. Minds that have been blinded by the devil will insist that God is not a healer, a way-maker, a peace-giver, a problem-solver, or a burden-bearer. If they choose the world over God, that is their choice. As children of God, we choose to believe.

11
Recognizing the Devil

But when he had turned about and looked on his disciples, he rebuked Peter, saying, Get thee behind me, Satan: for thou savourest not the things that be of God, but the things that be of men.

Mark 8:33

IN THE ABOVE scripture Jesus spoke to the spirit of the devil in Peter, rebuking him and bringing him into submission. Having the knowledge that we encounter spiritual wickedness on this earthly journey puts us in the position to recognize the devil and to resist him. That knowledge comes through the Holy Spirit, who resides in the believer who does the will of God. We all have access to the Holy Spirit when we are obedient to the Word. In this age we had better stay on God's good side, because the wicked one and his followers are on the prowl and full of evil.

The unwise person who lives for the moment, in the here and now, having his eyes focused on the world, is like a deer during archery hunting season, feasting on the grass even as the hunter dressed in camouflage aims his deadly weapon, and shoots and kills the deer, which was simply enjoying the fruits of this world and unaware the hunter was even there. Satan has tactics he uses to grab the world's attention. People of the world don't see the traps the sneaky one has set, and they walk right into them, because they are focused on the fireworks of the devil and not on the Word of God. Mankind chases after what the world considers important and neglects God, because men are living in the now with no regard for the hereafter. Before they know it, the devil has come to usher them to the grave.

The devil is telling people they have to worry. I remember working with a group of pleasant individuals in the service industry. One evening in the kitchen, the young man in our group was having a conversation with the older woman about how she was constantly worried about her daughter. The young man said, "You shouldn't worry yourself like that." She looked at him like he had called her some derogatory name. With disgust in her voice, she responded, "Why do you say I shouldn't worry? I do have to worry." She was bothered. I felt pity for her, as I thought she was carrying a heavy burden. The older woman was not alone in her thinking, though. Many people truly believe that they have to worry and that it is a good thing to worry. They are right where Satan wants them. To worry like that means their faith is not in God. They are shortsighted and the devil is laughing, saying, "I got you." The father of lies is on the loose, and his con game is as successful as ever.

Imagine going to the zoo and a hungry lion escapes. What is that famished and previously caged lion going to do? More than likely, it will roar and flash its sharp teeth and chase down the closest human in sight with the purpose of feeding on his flesh. The devil is like that, except he may attempt to disguise himself. Still, his goal remains the same: he is looking for unsuspecting victims to destroy by any means necessary. The devil traps us while we are in the dark. When we walk in the dark, we are no match for the wicked one. That is why recognizing him will be to our benefit as we travel through this world, which will one day pass away.

If we want to recognize the devil and those carrying out his plan of destruction, we cannot trust that devilish soldiers will be readily identifiable. When we are sick, they can come to us as caregivers. When we are in trouble, they can come to us as attorneys. In times of need, they can come to us as someone looking to meet our needs. And for a time, they may actually do so! Should we desire power, esteem, and great financial wealth, the devil will make sure we attain them. Yes, being the god of this world, he can grant us the fleeting desires of the flesh. In times of desperation, the devil's soldiers can come as saviors offering to satisfy whatever it is we are lacking and craving.

Satan's chosen can come to us with the knowledge of God and offer us soothing words. But they are not *of God*. Jesus warned us to "beware of false prophets, which come to you in sheep's clothing, but inwardly they are ravening wolves" (Matt. 7:15). Satan sends out an army that is well prepared to lead the unknowing down the path of destruction. Jesus also said, "Ye shall know them by their fruits" (v. 16). Our spiritual eyes must be wide open for us to see through their false identities.

People are hurting. The devil knows that. Believers and unbelievers alike are looking to the world for answers. The wicked one is well aware that we want answers, so he uses those who love evil to set traps. Those working for the devil will use scriptures to gain entry into the lives of the unsuspecting. Then they weave their webs of deceit. The workers of evil are then able to cause destruction.

The Word of God states, "Beloved, believe not every spirit, but try the spirits whether they are of God: because many false prophets are gone out into the world" (1 John 4:1). Notice that we are instructed to try—test—the spirits! That means we are to try the spirits that call themselves ministers, children of God, prophets and prophetesses, the ones who say that God is the head of their lives, deacons, and every person who claims to be sent in the name of the Lord. The church and the pulpit are filled with false prophets. It is not enough to take their word for who they claim to be. Listen to their words and observe their actions, and then compare your findings to the gospel of truth. Not every spirit has come in the name of the Lord. "And every spirit that confesseth not that Jesus Christ is come in the flesh is not of God: and this is that spirit of antichrist, whereof ye have heard that it should come; and even now already is it in the world" (v. 3). Remember Ephesians 6:12 from earlier? "For we wrestle not against flesh and blood, but against principalities, against powers, against the rulers of the darkness of this world, against spiritual wickedness in high places." We are not in a fight against people! We are wrestling with the rulers of the darkness of this world and with wicked spirits in high places. Paul said, "Prove all things; hold fast that which is good. Abstain from all appearance of evil" (1 Thess. 5:21-22).

We are often deceived by looks. If something looks good, we are all over it. We are living in and for the world, so we are easily duped into believing just about anything, especially when we do not want to believe otherwise. All it takes is a little bit of convincing sealed with a smile that comes off as genuine, plus some praise and whatever else we value in this world. We are unable to recognize the devil's deals because we are so easily taken with outer appearances and fast talking. If it looks good and sounds good to the flesh, and we are walking according to the flesh, we accept it without question. Therein lie the dangers of the devil.

The devil has many ways of getting willing participants to work for him, some with no knowledge that they are doing the work of the devil. Few people will admit they are evil and enjoy being evil. And some evil people don't seem to know they're evil. The devil isn't usually going to call himself "the devil" to us. If he did, he probably wouldn't be so successful at persuading individuals to engage in crimes against their neighbors or in persuading the wrong that they are right. Don't underestimate the devil's power to con, though. He can pull a con game so quickly, it can make our heads swim in confusion. We will be left sulking in our own foolishness.

Satan has an arsenal of weapons he uses to accomplish his entrapment of man. He uses tactics like cunning and trickery with ease. When the devil cons someone, that person actually believes he's done the right thing, no matter how wrong it might be. Satan paints a picture that looks pretty and inviting. This pretty picture entices us and makes us curious to want to know more. But once we take the bait, he's got us. He is the master of trickery who leads his prey down a path that seems right. The devil knows that man relies on his own weak wisdom to decide which path seems best.

The moves we make apart from God ensure that the devil's traps will be effective in bringing down those of us who trust in our own knowledge. We tend to grow bitter and resentful when this happens, and it's difficult to come to the realization that we're in our current situation because we've made an unwise decision and now we're separated from God. The prince of darkness stands at the helm of all bad things that happen to us. But he's crafty enough to fool the world into believing every evil act that takes place occurs simply because the people involved are evil on their own and responsible for their own actions—and it has nothing at all to do with this imaginary Satan person. In essence the children of the devil are saying that the Word of God is a lie. Because so many people believe that Satan is not responsible for the evil throughout the world, he can hide in plain sight.

Satan's spirit is everywhere we go in the world. His spirit travels through the wicked. We will inevitably come into contact with his earthly soldiers, whose sole purpose is to cause as much damage as possible. Many of the devil's soldiers are out in the open. They have sold their souls to the devil and have made up their minds to live the rest of their days for him. Others remain hidden, wearing sheep's clothing and plotting their attacks in secret. But we do not have to be afraid of these folks. These destroyers are identifiable regardless of what disguises they wear. Satan's attacks will not lead to total destruction in the lives of the spiritually connected. Our fraud detectors are in full working order.

God has left us with the Bible, which is our book of instruction on how to live a righteous, productive, enriching, and full life. It is our driver's manual. It tells us what signs to turn away from. We can hold the Bible up against any person to see if he or she be of God or of Satan. If we are deceived, it is our own fault. If the devil is successful in our lives, it is because we are neglecting to tap into the knowledge of Jesus Christ, who has defeated the enemy on our behalf. An alert child of God will survive and overcome the devil's attacks. Entertaining darkness throughout life, though, will cost us our eternal lives.

The Spirit of God is good and bears good fruit. The apostle Paul taught, "For the fruit of the Spirit is in all goodness and righteousness and truth" (Eph. 5:9). The things of God will be carried out by the people of God. With God's Spirit in us, love will be at the forefront of everything we do. Paul also said, "But the fruit of the Spirit is love, joy, peace, longsuffering, gentleness, goodness, faith, Meekness, temperance ..." (Gal. 5:22-23). The soul that lacks these fruits is the soul that lacks the knowledge of the Holy One. From him, run away!

Whatever we do, we have to hold the scriptures in our hearts and guard ourselves against evil and evildoers. We will face times when the devil and his workers try to set traps for us believers. They will come to us, talking about the scripture and about God. We must pay attention and not be fooled by every person claiming to know God. Satan believes in God too. His workers know enough about God and the Word of God to use it to their advantage to gain entry into lives of disobedient believers. James said that "the devils also believe" there is one God "and tremble" (2:19). So do not buy into someone's words about how much they believe in and love God. Again, observe them and test their actions against scripture. Jesus warned us that "Not every one that saith unto me, Lord, Lord, shall enter into the kingdom of heaven; but he that doeth the will of my Father which is in heaven" (Matt. 7:21).

Anybody can quote the Word. Anybody can call out the Lord's name. People do it all the time, all the while failing to do the will of God. Believers are only children of the Spirit if they are keepers of God's commandments. Children of God are commanded to stand out in a way that is acceptable to God. The apostle Paul wrote, "For it is God which worketh in you both to will and to do of his good pleasure" (Phil. 2:13). Paul then gave specific instructions about how to live godly lives in a world filled with darkness: "Do all things without murmurings and disputings: That ye may be blameless and harmless, the sons of God, without rebuke, in the midst of a crooked and perverse nation, among whom ye shine as lights in the world" (vv. 14-15). That is it! We have to be the lights in the world. We have to do good, keep the commandments, and model godly behavior. That is what will separate the children of God from the children of Satan.

12
How the Devil Wins

IF YOU HAVE made it this far in this book, you have some awareness of how the devil wins the spiritual fight for our souls. You may even have put together a list of things you need to do to keep the devil at a distance. Your list is either in your head or you have written it down on paper. As long as you hold that list in your heart and plant it in your spirit, you will not forget it.

You have now read about who Satan is, what his plan is for us, and how to identify him even when he is, so to speak, dressed in sheep's clothing and looks like the rest of us. He is on the lookout for us. He wants to trip us up in this world, to steal our joy, happiness, and hope. He wants to kill our dreams and our spirit. He wants to destroy our careers, our finances, our families, our relationships with our fellow man, and to ruin every part of our lives.

But the fallen angel knows what his end will be. The Bible tells us so. The scripture says, "Woe to the inhabiters of the earth and of the sea! for the devil is come down unto you, having great wrath, because he knoweth that he hath but a short time" (Rev. 12:12). Satan understands the misery that is to come his way. This is why he needs company. He doesn't want to suffer alone in the bottomless pit. So he is making his way through the world, taking it by storm and, one by one, winning many souls in the process.

It is no secret that the thief is sprinting happily toward the finish line, knowing there will be many receiving the same sentence as he, although he will be in total misery once his sentence is handed down. His sentence: chained to the bottomless pit forever. The many souls he has stolen are nothing compared to the total number of lives he will claim before the end of the world. The father of lies has deceived the world. His body count is enormous. He is so successful because the souls he steals are willing participants in their own destruction.

Examine the state of the world, if you will. See how the devil is winning the fight, how he is winning souls left and right! "How," you ask, "does the devil win?" The answer: he is so skillful at making things that are detrimental to us appear "right" or "desirable" or "exciting." He makes it seem as if we cannot live without the very things that cause us the most harm. That's what he does best. Just when we've gotten in over our heads with the wrong things, he pulls the greatest trick of all out of his hat—*illusion*, in which lies take on the appearance of things real and true. The great deceiver traps us and then goes in for the kill. He wins by default, really— because we give up without a fight. We cannot see that our Helper is reaching out to us, offering to pull us out of the pit. When the devil has stolen our hope, all we see is ashes.

The devil wins in many ways. He knows that man is arrogant and puffed up. He knows that man denies the power of God and trusts in his own worldly wisdom. The con artist

Satan is aware of this and uses it to his advantage. By making worldly wisdom the gospel that the majority of people in the world live by today, the devil is able to keep on destroying lives and claiming souls.

God was aware of man's foolishness from the beginning. He knew how man would cash in on his own foolishness in a world so desperate for answers that people will believe anything that makes them feel good. Often the more educated in the world a man becomes, the more he uses wisdom gained from the world to refute the gospel of Jesus Christ and the existence of the Almighty God. Satan wins here too.

Worldly wisdom is not the same as God's wisdom. This is why we were forewarned concerning the worldly wisdom that so many of us presently live by. The apostle Paul asserted, "Let no man deceive himself. If any man among you seemeth to be wise in this world, let him become a fool, that he may be wise. For the wisdom of this world is foolishness with God. For it is written, He taketh the wise in their own craftiness" (1 Cor. 3:18-19).

Man is too often a know-it-all who thinks he has all the answers to life's issues. He fails to trust in the true gospel that God provided to teach and guide us along the way. When men abide in worldly, human wisdom, the devil will always come out the winner. The serpent laughs because he knows he is able to use man's arrogance against him, because man is always ready to believe his own foolishness. Although man's wisdom governs the world of unbelievers, it will never hold up against the Word of God.

God's divine instruction telling man not to deceive himself could not be more vital in this current age. If we pay close attention to the theories drafted and adopted by people in the fields of education, psychology, science, criminology, sociology, and similar arenas, and also look at the ever-diminishing condition of societies across the planet, we ought to be able to clearly see that the wisdom of man (both educated and uneducated) is foolishness. It has failed to bring healing to the world. Of course this is no secret. Man is "ever learning, and never able to come to the knowledge of the truth" (2 Tim. 3:7). Man is his own think tank and relies on his own version of truth. He throws aside the truth of the gospel. In so doing, the devil wins again.

Because human beings are so stubborn and set in their faulty ways, they will self-destruct. Thus we see the arrogance of man. He will not give up his position, even though it may be wrong and detrimental to himself and to others. Man's wisdom should not hold weight, but it is used, unfortunately, to run the world. This foolishness captivates people. The world hangs on to man's every word and suggestion. Civilizations fall at the hands of the unwise and those who lack understanding. Schools are failing large segments of society. World leaders are unable to find the solutions to society's ills. They are now part of the ongoing decay of societies. Religious leaders and churches continue to be divided. This is all caused by the failure of man, a sad result of how he has exalted his abilities above God.

Whatever happened to the question, "What would Jesus do?" Does anyone stop and ask this anymore? It is safe to say that the question has been replaced with, "I know what's best for me and for society." Foolishness blinds us. The great deceiver is watching us and saying, "I've got them right where I want them." He's right! Satan is winning small battles every day. We see this, but we do not attribute these victories to him. The devil has people scratching their heads and running around in circles, trying to figure out how to stop the violence served up like a three-course meal, seven days a week, twenty-four hours a day. Man is looking for what he can see while the spirit of wickedness goes unnoticed.

The reason things are not going to get any better, and the world remains in such a great state of chaos, is that we are not banding together in the name of Jesus, serving and obeying God, praying for His divine intervention, and loving Him and trusting in Him with our whole heart. We are pulling away from God and dancing with demons, loving things and status and reputation more than we are loving each other. We have gone our own way as we try to figure out how to live in the world on our own. The devil and his army walk away with the win.

Put this in your spirit: *God's truth is absolute.* But the devil will continue to win souls due to our unbelief. Although he will prevail in some battles, the war is already won. Jesus made sure of it when He died on the cross for our sins. Satan knows this too. Even though he is operating like he is victorious, the truth is that Satan is already defeated. He cannot win against us unless we allow it to happen. The cunning one will succeed in wiping out families and societies, but only because he is allowed to do so. The devil wins when people turn away from God and dwell in the flesh.

But we have a choice! We can claim the power of God over our lives and live for Him. Or we can forsake God and ride with the devil, accepting temporary earthly pleasures in exchange for eternal damnation. Which will it be?

13
What Sorrows Will Come

*And Jesus answered and said unto them, Take
heed that no man deceive you. For many shall
come in my name, saying, I am Christ; and shall
deceive many. And ye shall hear of wars and
rumours of wars: see that ye be not troubled: for
all these things must come to pass, but the end
is not yet. For nation shall rise against nation,
and kingdom against kingdom: and there shall be
famines, and pestilences, and earthquakes, in div-
ers places. All these are the beginning of sorrows.*

Matt. 24:4-8

FOR AGES MAN has been wondering and guessing when
the end of time will come. During the latter part of 1999, I
received countless reports on television, in the newspapers,
on front porches, in grocery stores, and all around town that

the world would end on January 1, 2000. Food was flying off the shelves. People were building storm-proof spaces they thought would keep them safe from the end. Predictions had been made that the end was right around the corner. This wasn't the first time man had made such foolish predictions. Man is always making erroneous predictions.

End-of-time predictions cause panic all over the world. The unwise believe these predictions of psychics and anyone they feel has knowledge of when the end will come. With that information they run around—deceiving and being deceived. But the chaos and confusion that the living will experience in the times ahead will make the turmoil brought about by previous end-of-world predictions seem tame.

Can you remember what happened on January 1, 2000? Life went on as usual, did it not? Again, man's predictions were wrong. God's people did not panic (mostly). They laughed and then they cried at how out of touch their neighbors were when it came to the gospel of truth. We know that God is the only One who knows when the end of time will be.

It is useless for any man to try to determine when the end of time will come upon us. Yes, predicting the end of this world garners a lot of attention, as well as a lot of believers. But anyone who claims to know that date is speaking lies. Man's estimation of the end times is foolishness, and he will pay a steep price for leading people astray. The man who says the world will end on a specific date is a liar who chooses to pervert the Word of God. Various men have predicted the end of the world, and every time the world has continued to move right along.

You'd think that God's Word would at some point prevail as the authority on when the world will end. But it has not.

People are still guessing and still making a mockery of themselves. As Jesus taught, "But of that day and hour knoweth no man, no, not even the angels of heaven, but my Father only" (Matt. 24:36). Please, whatever you do, let that truth sink in. Stop allowing man to trick you! Man has no knowledge of such a time. The individual who says he can predict the end of time is of the devil. The truth is not in him.

Events are happening and are going to happen to let us know that we are living in the end times. The world will bear witness to great suffering—confusion and chaos, wars and rumors of wars, horrible and fatal diseases, and plagues, famines, and earthquakes. Things will not get any better from that point onward. Troubles and suffering will increase. Jesus said that there "shall be great tribulation, such as was not since the beginning of the world to this time, no, nor ever shall be" (Matt. 24:21). Picture the great tribulation for a moment. We have seen nothing like it! But can you imagine things getting any worse than they already are? Whether we can imagine it or not, it is going to happen. Those in Christ, though, will not be moved to fear.

In this present time the state of the world is whirling in a downward spiral. Hate is increasing, murders are increasing, wars are happening in all parts of the world. Neighbors are warring against neighbors, gang against gang, political parties against each other, country against country. There are rumors of race wars. Civil unrest is boiling over like an erupting volcano. Mankind will fall victim to an abundance of diseases—old diseases, new diseases, "mysterious" diseases. These will destroy health, take away independence, and claim lives. Diseases will arise and make AIDS and cancer *seem* tame and almost harmless. The times are showing us that the

Word of God is being fulfilled. BUT THE END HAS NOT YET ARRIVED!

The spiritually wicked are fighting to remove God from everything. Satan wants to wipe God from our minds for good. The devil has many agents willing to destroy any sign of God. As Paul wrote, "For the time will come when they will not endure sound doctrine; but after their own lusts shall they heap to themselves teachers, having itching ears; And they shall turn away their ears from the truth, and shall be turned unto fables" (2 Tim. 4:3-4). Turning away from God is death.

We are living in the last days. The spirit of the devil is running throughout the world, infecting the lost. The lost are running around in circles, unaware. Children are being lost to the streets, choosing to live lives of crime, forsaking what is good. They are being lured away by the enemy. They despise and reject the gospel of Christ and follow the devil.

"In the last days," the apostle Paul also wrote, "perilous times shall come" (2 Tim. 3:1). Then Paul gave us a list of evils that are to come:

> For men shall be lovers of their own selves, covetous, boasters, proud, blasphemers, disobedient to parents, unthankful, unholy, Without natural affection, trucebreakers, false accusers, incontinent, fierce, despisers of those that are good, Traitors, heady, highminded, lovers of pleasures more than lovers of God; Having a form of godliness, but denying the power thereof: from such turn away. (vv. 2-5)

All those things are happening right now. Those sins are fast becoming the new normal. This will happen on an even more devastating scale. Believers are warned to turn away from these workers of iniquity. Although the end times will be trying times, God will give the obedient everything they need to survive and to thrive.

This fallen world in which we live will go on decaying. Sorrows will rain down upon mankind with terrifying consequences. Our days are numbered, but we cannot even try to guess when the end will come, for that knowledge has not been given to us. The best we can do is to be ready when that day comes. In the meantime we must hold on and endure the trials and tribulations we will no doubt have to face.

As Jesus said, "… because iniquity shall abound, the love of many shall wax cold" (Matt. 24:12). Some may ask, "Will the great tribulation wipe out every person left on earth?" No, it will not. Jesus comforted us with these words: "And except those days should be shortened, there should no flesh be saved: but for the elect's sake those days shall be shortened" (v. 22). In all the tribulations that are to come, we can have hope at the end of sorrow. Jesus told us that those times will not be a walk in the park, but also that they will not last forever. That is why He encourages us to ride out the storms until the end.

To avoid being led down the path of destruction, we have to be able to read the signs of the times. Many of us will be led down that path of destruction because we will not accept the truth. The Bible teaches that "there shall arise false Christs, and false prophets, and shall shew great signs and wonders …" (v. 24). Just how great will those signs and wonders be? The answer is given in the same verse: "… insomuch that, if it were possible, they shall deceive the very elect" (v. 24). We are not to be tricked by their amazing fireworks, and we can be assured that Satan will present many wonders to distract the lost. But God is with the faithful believer.

14

How to Win against the Evil One

AS IN ANY fight or war, it is mandatory that an opponent knows who the enemy is, where he is, and what his tactics are. In this spiritual war the enemy has pushed the button on the weapons of mass destruction. We, the targets, must be able to recognize every human being who is working to help the enemy divide and conquer. Entering the ring unprepared and with no idea how the opponent operates will set us up for defeat every time. To know who the enemy is, our homework has to be done, and it has to be accurate.

The commander in chief of all wickedness and all demonic spirits has given his army orders to increase his kingdom. And they have been deployed to our location. Demonic spirits have entered men, women, and children who walk in darkness, because they are willing to commit evil deeds against their neighbors. No good works come from the sons and daughters of the chief of demons. The rulers of darkness want us to believe this war is all about man and what we can see. It is not about man, because man is just the vessel used to achieve high-level evil that cannot be seen with the eyes.

One more time, in case you forgot: this war is spiritual. To win the war against the powers of darkness, we are going to need to know and to believe that the evil happening in this world is not without a powerful leader. Our weapons, to be effective, have to be spiritual ones that God has ordained.

We will never win a war with the devil if we walk around believing we are warring against people who just happen to be "bad." If that were the case, the war against evil would probably have been won hundreds of years ago. It is our denial of the gospel of Jesus Christ that has gotten us to this low point. We are running around fighting one another in vain, even as the devil walks away unseen and unbothered.

"Submit yourselves therefore to God. Resist the devil, and he will flee from you" (James 4:7). Winning the fight against spiritual wickedness and all temptations of evil requires that we do some serious work. We have to open our hearts to God and obey His Word, even though Satan will continue to hinder us and tempt us on our journey through the valley of the shadow of death. When we submit ourselves to the ways of God, the Holy Spirit will guide us away from harm and danger. We are required to live a certain way to gain the power to resist and rebuke the devil. In addition we also have to be willing to sacrifice the flesh. That is, we have to resist the urge to go our own way and indulge in the sinful pleasures of this world.

There is no quicker way to succumb to the devil's tricks than to believe there is no God. Living in a state of unbelief is like walking blindfolded down a dark path filled with land mines. At any given moment we will step on a mine, and it will claim our physical lives as well as our souls. The believer who does the will of God will not be without challenges, of course, but he will not be put to shame. He will be saved from destruction and the second death. God will save the just. How can we be saved from the second death? Belief in God and His Word is a step in the right direction. We have to carry the truth in our hearts—that God sent Jesus Christ, His Son, to die for our sins.

Endurance is required in the battle against the rulers of darkness. Endurance is key to surviving the attacks of the devil and keeping our hearts and minds intact. Without endurance we will be weak. We will give in to the situations that try us, and then give up. We all know someone who has given up because he or she could not see God due to their focus on their disappointments, letdowns, and troubles. As exercise increases our physical endurance and gives us the strength and power to get through physically demanding tasks, so studying the gospel allows God's Word to build us up, give us strength in times of trouble, and provide us power to overcome the world and its delusions.

It's true that there will be temptations and trials throughout this life. We will be tempted to follow the world in order to gain the approval of others. Trials will come to test our patience and our faith. Some trials will tempt us to fall into bitterness and hate. Other trials will be so severe that they will cause many to put an end to their own lives. We see this every day, as old and young folks alike see their trials as being larger than life, so they commit suicide. Or they commit murder. They simply give up, feeling they cannot endure any longer. I love what the gospel says about enduring temptation: "Blessed is the man that endureth temptation: for when he is tried, he shall receive the crown of life, which the Lord hath promised to them that love him" (James 1:12). Every time I read that verse, I feel I can go another day. You want to talk about something giving you life? Then talk about the goodness of the Lord and His promises.

To love God is to do His will. When we do His will, He promises to take care of us, to give us everything we need, and to see us successfully through this wicked world. God will save His children from eternal defeat. God promises that if we "shall endure unto the end, the same shall be saved" (Matt. 24:13). Get the message? We have to endure. God would not have told us to endure if He hadn't given us the power to do so.

As long as we are among the living, evil will be here to oppose us, to wear us down, and to steal our hope and joy. This is why we must be protected by special armor as we go to battle against spiritual wickedness and rulers of the darkness. The armor, when worn by believers who do the will of God, is strong enough that even the prince of the power of the air cannot penetrate it with any lasting, damaging effect. Paul advised, "Put on the whole armour of God, that ye may be able to stand against the wiles of the devil" (Eph. 6:11). Without this protective gear, we are sitting ducks in an open field, where every season is hunting season. Once we don that suit of godly armor, though, the devil has no power to win against us.

To stand victorious in these evil times, our feet have to be planted on solid ground, and we must stand in the light, with our "loins girt about with truth, and having on the breastplate of righteous" (Eph. 6:14). It boils down to this: it is mandatory that our hearts and minds be protected so that neither evil nor lies can enter in and settle in us. Our faith and belief in the gospel of the Savior cannot waver. Jesus Christ is the way to God's kingdom, and that truth has to be buried so deeply inside us that no man will be able to convince us otherwise.

To rise above the enemy, we also have to be prepared to go about the world spreading the good news. Paul stressed that our "feet" be "shod with the preparation of the gospel of peace" (Eph. 6:15). As God's missionaries and ministers, we are responsible for spreading the good news wherever we go. The gospel provides peace to all who believe. The gospel instructs us also to live peaceably with one another and to live holy. The writer of Hebrews preached, "Follow peace with all men, and holiness, without which no man shall see the Lord" (12:14).

Peace among people is enormously lacking in these current times. Millions of people are at odds with each other, and chaos is the climate across the world. And Satan is loving it! He wins during times like these. This is why true believers must stand tall and walk in the light and do everything we can to encourage peace. The gospel of peace teaches this important lesson: "See that none render evil for evil unto any man; but ever follow that which is good, both among yourselves, and to all men" (1 Thess. 5:15). We believers are to "Preach the word; be instant in season, out of season; reprove, rebuke, exhort with all long suffering and doctrine" (2 Tim. 4:2).

Winning this spiritual war requires faith in God, which pleases Him. Thus Paul also encouraged us, "above all," to take "the shield of faith, wherewith [we] shall be able to quench all the fiery darts of the wicked" (Eph. 6:16). Our success against evil is dependent upon our faith and our efforts to grow nearer to God, our protector. Faith gives us hope. If there is no hope, we believe that we have already lost. Faith is trust. "Every word of God is pure: he is a shield unto them that put their trust in him" (Prov. 30:5). Trust in God gives us a shield of protection that the enemy cannot penetrate. Our faith in God is how we defeat the devil. Hide the following truths in your heart:

> Whosoever believeth that Jesus is the Christ is born of God: and every one that loveth him that begat loveth him also that is begotten of him. By this we know that we love the children of God, when we love God, and keep his commandments. For this is the love of God, that we keep his commandments: and his commandments are not grievous. For whatsoever is born of God overcometh the world: and this is the victory that overcometh the world, even our faith. Who is he that overcometh the world, but he that believeth that Jesus is the Son of God? … For there are three that bear record in heaven, the Father, the Word, and the Holy Ghost: and these three are one. (1 John 5:1-5, 7)

Two more pieces of gear are needed to complete dressing in the whole armor of God: "Take the helmet of salvation, and the sword of the Spirit, which is the word of God" (Eph. 6:17). Walking through this fallen world means we will no doubt be attacked by evil. Accepting Jesus as our Lord and Savior is the helmet that protects our minds from the untruths that the father of lies will present to us. Walking in truth equips us with the sword that will cut through the thick darkness and smite the evildoers that dare to come against us. Having on the full armor of God is how we win. No holes, no demons!

15
God Is Coming: What We Can Expect

And, behold, I come quickly; and my reward is with me, to give every man according as his work shall be.

Rev. 22:12

GOD IS COMING! For His children, oh, what a day this will be. I, for one, look forward to the day of Jesus's return. "For as the lightning cometh out of the east, and shineth even unto the west; so shall also the coming of the Son of man be" (Matt. 24:27). What a sight that is going to be, Jesus coming in all His majesty and power, with the book of life in His hand. The book of life will be opened, and everyone will be judged according to all they have done on earth (Rev. 20:12-13). Life and death are in His hands, and every man will receive one or the other.

Jesus compared His coming to how "the days of Noah were" (Matt. 24:37). In the days of Noah, man "knew not until the flood came, and took them all away; so shall also the coming of the Son of man be" (v. 39). The masses will be engaging in normal activities without any thought of God. Can you picture them throwing parties, drinking and dancing and celebrating birthdays, weddings, anniversaries, and job promotions—doing all of this without God ever entering into their thought processes and without regard to getting their souls right with Him? Like the generation of Noah, they will be taken away in their sin, because they will have lived a lie, having denied the gospel of Jesus Christ. The coming of Jesus is going to catch people off guard, even though scripture warns that we should be ready at all times.

The first coming of Jesus was epic. He was the Word of God made flesh, and His purpose was to spread the gospel to all who would hear it, and to die for our sins. Jesus walked the earth, healing the sick, casting out demons, feeding the poor, guiding people to the light, giving hope to and fighting for the oppressed. He did not come to judge the world, but to heal it. He came to give men and women access to eternal life. Jesus explained why He was sent:

> The Spirit of the Lord is upon me, because he hath anointed me to preach the gospel to the poor; he hath sent me to heal the brokenhearted, to preach deliverance to the captives, and recovering of sight to the blind, to set at liberty them that are bruised, To preach the acceptable year of the Lord. (Luke 4:18-19)

During Jesus's time on earth, His mission was to offer salva-tion to the lost, ultimately dying for all sinners so that we may have eternal life. That mission was accomplished when Jesus died on Calvary's cross and arose with full power in His hands. Yet multitudes of people say He's dead forever. Some even say He was just another man. And still others say He never lived at all.

When we consider the abundance of horrors occurring every hour of every day, it's easy to ask ourselves, "Where is God?" or "Is God real?" Throughout the world people are ask-ing, "Why is God allowing all these tragedies to take place?" Even more people are saying, "With all the suffering in the world, there couldn't possibly be a God." Mankind seems to believe we are living in a godless world in which we are left on our own to fend for ourselves. That's what the devil wants us to believe, because a deceived world is a hopeless and power-less world.

We've read that Satan is the god of this world. Nevertheless God is here, right now, even as you are reading this book. And let's not forget that "God is our refuge and strength, a very present help in trouble" (Ps. 46:1). This scripture tells us that God is here for us—right now! Our questioning God's exis-tence is directly related to our unbelief.

God is present and available to us, despite any word to the contrary! He loves us and has not left us to fend for ourselves. God is waiting for us, if only we'd ask Him to come into our hearts. Jesus promised, "Ask, and it shall be given you; seek, and ye shall find; knock, and it shall be opened unto you: For every one that asketh receiveth; and he that seeketh findeth; and to him that knocketh it shall be opened" (Matt. 7:7-8).

And Psalm 34:18 assures that "the Lᴏʀᴅ is nigh unto them that are of a broken heart; and saveth such as be of a contrite spirit." Yes, the Lord is here already, and He is close to the righteous! "The righteous cry, and the Lᴏʀᴅ heareth, and delivereth them out of all their troubles" (v. 17). Isn't it a wonderful feeling to know that when we are blameless before God, He will rescue us out of the hands of the wicked? He will save those of us who have a repentant heart.

Just as a loving father comes to his child's rescue, God is coming to rescue us, His children, from the injustices and struggles that burden us in this present life. He is also coming to separate the true believers from the wicked. When God gave His Son Jesus to the world, I'm sure it pained Him to know what Jesus would have to endure so that our sins could be forgiven. God did it for us. This means He has our best interests at heart.

Before Jesus's second return, trials and tribulations will continue all over the planet. We believers will have to endure and not fear whatever may befall us. In the absence of Jesus being physically present on earth, God has sent to us the Holy Ghost, who is our comforter and our guide. God the Father was well aware that those of us left here on earth would face difficulties, temptations, and hindrances. The times would not get any better and we would grow more distant from Him before His second coming.

The first coming of Jesus Christ might have been epic and life-changing, but the second coming will be apocalyptic. Let us not make the mistake of separating God the Father from God the Son, who is Jesus! Jesus and the Father are One. Jesus said, "If ye had known me, ye should have known the Father also: and from henceforth ye know him, and have seen him"

(John 14:7). So when Jesus makes His second appearance, it will be in the full power of the Father. He will not be coming to die for us again or to save us from our sins. That's already been done.

This time Jesus will be coming to gather up the righteous and to condemn the wicked. The Word of God asks a question about the one who condemns and then answers it: "Who is he that condemneth? It is Christ that died, yea rather, that is risen again, who is even at the right hand of God, who also maketh intercession for us" (Rom. 8:34). Jesus will return as the judge carrying the keys to heaven and hell. He will be claiming some of us as His own and rejecting others who served the god of this age. The only way to be a part of the flock to whom God grants eternal life is to accept Jesus as our Lord and Savior.

Upon Jesus's second coming, we can expect final judgment. The apostle Paul asserted, "For we must all appear before the judgment seat of Christ; that every one may receive the things done in his body, according to that he hath done, whether it be good or bad" (2 Cor. 5:10). None will escape the judgment seat of Christ. Neither lies nor excuses will save us. There will be no deceiving Jesus, who knows everything we have ever done and everything we shall ever do. And have no doubts about it—Jesus will be the One rendering our just deserts at the judgment: "For the Father judgeth no man, but hath committed all judgment unto the Son" (John 5:22).

"He that heareth my word, and believeth on him that sent me, hath everlasting life, and shall not come into condemnation; but is passed from death unto life" (John 5:24). Those are Jesus's words. He is the Word and cannot lie. Believers who abide by God's commandments will not face condemnation. God is going to gather to Himself those who "believe that

Jesus died and rose again, even so them also which sleep in Jesus will God bring with him" (1 Thess. 4:14). Jesus's coming will be glorious and magnificent: "For the Lord himself shall descend from heaven with a shout, with the voice of the archangel, and with the trump of God: and the dead in Christ shall rise first" (v. 16). According to the Word of God, after the dead in Christ have risen, those "which are alive and remain shall be caught up together with them in the clouds, to meet the Lord in the air: and so shall we ever be with the Lord" (v. 17).

In the end Satan will be judged. This will be the final judgment against the one who has deceived the world. Satan and all his demons will meet their end. For their final dwelling place, God has reserved the bottomless pit. The revelation is this: "And the devil that deceived them was cast into the lake of fire and brimstone, where the beast and the false prophet are, and shall be tormented day and night for ever and ever" (Rev. 20:10). That sounds like nothing I want to be a part of. How about you?

With the end of wickedness, suffering will become a thing of the past. The righteous will cry no more. The unrighteous will perish: "... at the end of the world: the angels shall come forth, and sever the wicked from among the just, And shall cast them into the furnace of fire: there shall be wailing and gnashing of teeth" (Matt. 13:49-50). It's going to be a terrifying time for people who rejected the truth of the gospel. They will cry day and night, and will not be heard nor comforted. Suffering will go on forever and ever. Evildoers will be shut out of the kingdom of God. The following people will experience the second death: "the fearful, and unbelieving, and the abominable, and murderers, and whoremongers, and sorcerers, and idolaters, and all liars" (Rev. 21:8). God said it. It shall be done. These will be devastating times for unbelievers who traded an eternity with God for temporary, earthly pleasures. There will be no more opportunities to get it right.

People who were tricked by the devil into believing they have done all the right things to get into heaven will be trying to make a case for themselves, saying, "Lord, Lord, have we not prophesied in thy name? and in thy name have cast out devils? and in thy name done many wonderful works? (Matt. 7:22). Can you see this taking place? People are going to try to finagle their way through the pearly gates. But Jesus is going to stop them dead in their lies and deceit. Jesus declared, "And then will I profess unto them, I never knew you: depart from me, ye that work iniquity" (v. 23). Those words will be final. I cannot fathom what it will feel like to hear those words. "And whosoever was not found written in the book of life was cast into the lake of fire" (Rev. 20:15).

Jesus will also call the names of the persons who endured until the end. Everlasting peace will be their inheritance. That inheritance will be far beyond any good thing we could have ever imagined. "But as it is written, Eye hath not seen, nor ear heard, neither have entered into the heart of man, the things which God hath prepared for them that love him" (1 Cor. 2:9). There will be "a new heaven and a new earth ... and ... no more sea" (Rev. 21:1). These will be joyous times for the children of God: "... the tabernacle of God [will be] with men, and he will dwell with them, and they shall be his people, and God himself shall be with them, and be their God" (v. 3). Satan, sin, and death will be defeated forever. Earthly troubles will be no more. These are the promises of God: "And God shall wipe away all tears from their eyes; and there shall be no more death, neither sorrow, nor crying, neither shall there be any more pain: for the former things are passed away" (v. 4). In our new home "there shall be no night there" (Rev. 22:5).

Amen and hallelujah! I long for that day, and I pray that you do as well. May the Lord who has offered us salvation through Christ give you peace and strength to endure until the end as you faithfully serve Him. His blessings be upon you!

www.ingramcontent.com/pod-product-compliance
Lightning Source LLC
Chambersburg PA
CBHW051831090426
42736CB00011B/1743